A POST-TRUTH WORLD

SELECTED BOOKS BY KEN WILBER

FINDING RADICAL WHOLENESS
The Integral Path to Unity, Growth, and Delight (2024)

A BRIEF HISTORY OF EVERYTHING
(20th Anniversary Edition), with a new afterword by
Lana Wachowski and Ken Wilber (2017)

THE RELIGION OF TOMORROW
A Vision of the Future of the Great Traditions—
More Inclusive, More Comprehensive, More Complete (2017)

INTEGRAL MEDITATION
Mindfulness as a Path to Grow Up,
Wake Up, and Show Up in Your Life (2016)

THE INTEGRAL VISION
A Very Short Introduction to the Revolutionary Integral
Approach to Life, God, the Universe, and Everything (2007)

A THEORY OF EVERYTHING
An Integral Vision for Business,
Politics, Science, and Spirituality (2000)

SEX, ECOLOGY, SPIRITUALITY
The Spirit of Evolution (1995)

GRACE AND GRIT
Spirituality and Healing in the
Life and Death of Treya Killam Wilber (1991)

A POST-TRUTH WORLD

POLITICS, POLARIZATION, *and a* VISION
for TRANSCENDING *the* CHAOS

Ken Wilber

SHAMBHALA

Shambhala Publications, Inc.
2129 13th Street
Boulder, Colorado 80302
www.shambhala.com

Cover art: Tupungato/Adobe Stock
Cover design: Daniel Urban-Brown

9 8 7 6 5 4 3 2 1

Second Edition
Printed in the United States of America

Shambhala Publications makes every effort to print on acid-free, recycled paper.
Shambhala Publications is distributed worldwide by Penguin Random House, Inc., and its subsidiaries.

LIBRARY OF CONGRESS CATALOGING-IN-PUBLICATION DATA
Names: Wilber, Ken, author.
Title: A post-truth world: politics, polarization, and a vision for transcending the chaos / Ken Wilber. Other titles: Trump and a post-truth world
Description: Second edition. | Boulder: Shambhala Publications, 2024. | Revised edition of: Trump and a post-truth world. Boulder: Shambhala, 2017.
Identifiers: LCCN 2023059625 | ISBN 9781645473558 (trade paperback)
Subjects: LCSH: United States—Politics and government—21st century. | Social evolution—Political aspects—United States. | Truthfulness and falsehood—Political aspects—United States. | Trump, Donald, 1946–
Classification: LCC JK275 .W52 2024 | DDC 973.933092—dc23/eng/20240118
LC record available at https://lccn.loc.gov/2023059625

Contents

Preface to the 2024 Edition

We are definitely living in tough times. One of the best chroniclers of these times is Douglas Murray, a well-known author and participant in television commentary shows. The titles of his major books say it all: *The Strange Death of Europe, The Madness of Crowds, The War on the West.* That last book, in some editions, has the subtitle: "How to Prevail in the Age of Unreason," which is true enough. Today's world is, in a sense, indeed an Age of Unreason, but it is harder to explain how this modern world just arose and came out of the immediately previous stage of development, which was universally called the Age of Reason. How did we manage to go so quickly and thoroughly from "reason" to "unreason"? Something—whatever it was—must have hit our culture like several tons of bricks falling at once.

Indeed, it did. First of all, these tons of bricks were actually several items, with one of them leading the pack. These several items included the gradual but rather widespread loss of any serious belief in our country's Judeo-Christian tradition. The most-clicked box in America today on polls asking "which religion do you believe in?" is the "none of the above" choice. Another huge influence on our civic attitudes is caused by the internet and so-called social media. Among other things, people will simply say rather nasty things either about or directly to a person when they are anonymous—as if they were actually wearing a mask (and all social media is anonymous, or mask-wearing). This process selects for interactions that are crude, vile, often mean-spirited, even vicious, and definitely irrational. National studies have shown that teens who use a significant amount of social media now have more anxiety, more depression, more suicide, and participate in more bullying. This "mental health epidemic" is being called by America's Surgeon General a national health care crisis. Plus, there's the added national zeitgeist in general, which also seems to have itself taken a sharp irrational downturn into glumness and depression.

All of those have a fully recognized hand in this downturn and have been spotted by many professionals and experts. But one super-significant factor has played a major hand in this affair—likely the biggest and most important hand—and yet it has not been recognized at all: the major role that developmental stages of human growth themselves have on these issues.

This of course takes a bit of explaining, and we will fully do so in the following chapters. For now, I'll simply say that perhaps the greatest discovery in modern psychology of the last one hundred years is the realization that all human beings—as they grow from birth and childhood through adolescence into young adulthood, middle adulthood, and old age—go through a series of exactly the same major stages of growth. These stages have been given different names by dozens of different researchers; a commonly used set of names is that given by the genius Jean Gebser who called them "the archaic stage," the "magic stage," the "mythic," the "rational," the "pluralistic," and the "systemic" or the "integral stage." Most individuals proceed through those developmental stages at particular time periods in their own lives, although the earlier stages are experienced by almost everybody at the same time: the archaic stage, the first year of life; the magic stage, years 2–5; the mythic stage, years 6–11; and then for most people, the rational stage emerges at some point in adolescence. Whether all of them develop further into the pluralistic or the integral stages varies among them. But the important role that these stages play in our recent irrational "downturn" (into the Age of Unreason) is that today is exactly the point when most Westerners are moving from the rational stage to the pluralistic stage. And from the names of those stages alone you can almost guess what the reason is (that is, from "rational" to "pluralistic").

Let's go back one step for a fuller explanation. As humans moved from the Magic Age to the great Mythic Age Era, it was indeed an age when mythology ruled. Everything in the universe was filled with mythic gods and goddesses and nature spirits. What these gods and goddesses got from the previous Magic Age was the power to perform magic—magic miracles, magic feats, magic healings, and magic crop bloomings. In this Mythic Era, humans themselves could no longer perform magical feats (which they believed they could in the previous Age of Magic), but the mythic-heavenly hosts, gods, and goddesses could perform all sorts of magical feats and miracles. And if you approached these mythic gods with the right attitude, they would respond appropriately—perhaps a prayer of thanks for making the crops grow, or possibly an animal sacrifice (or, during this Mythic Age, actual human sacrifice was fairly common).

But the primary Age of Myth itself (roughly 10,000 B.C.E. to 1,000 C.E.) was the time of the real full-blown emergence of the Great Religions—Judaism, Christianity, Islam, Vedanta Hinduism, Taoism, Buddhism. Hence, in all of these religions you generally find mythic gods or goddesses, or at least nature spirits (or some sort of human-nature spirit), with all sorts of spiritual practices (prayer, meditation, animal or human sacrifice) that will help put you directly in touch with these mythic spirits so as to more readily receive their boons. It's fair to say that virtually every human society on this planet went through some form or another of these types of religious beliefs, often written down throughout foundational textual traditions (the Bible, the Torah, the Tao Te Ching, the Vedas, the Sutras, and so forth)—and they did so because they all were going through exactly this mythic period of their own development.

Such was the general mythic-oriented form of civilization until the Middle Ages, which saw the emergence of various historical events that would indicate that the next available stage of human development—the rational stage—was about to emerge (and it got placed there by the rare but impactful evolutionary pioneers of the past). And thus, in the year 1605, both Galileo and Kepler simultaneously introduced the notion that the laws of nature are to be best understood through rational measurement. Galileo measured earthly motion and came up with his laws of terrestrial movement, and Kepler measured planetary motion and came up with his laws of planetary movement, and the super-genius Isaac Newton later put them all together and came up with his universal laws of force and gravity. All of these were the products of the rational stage of development—not one of them had a single god, goddess, or nature spirit in it. When Napoleon was shown a working model of what the solar system looked like with Newton's model, he conspicuously commented, "But there is no god in it." The reply came back: "Because it doesn't need one in order to work."

Thus was born the Age of Reason.

Because reason easily differentiates subject and object, most of the new sciences of the Age of Reason strove to be objective in nature. And likewise, human beings were understood to have a real subjective component, and thus came to be known as "human persons"—and most importantly, all persons have free rights (hence, the major emancipatory or slave-freeing movements came in the Age of Reason, especially starting in the 1800s). Technology itself became rational, and thus was adopted by people the world over, and this technology became more and more global as more people moved into the stage of rational development. The Age of Reason (and its technology) went largely worldwide and was happily adopted. For this reason, rationality was thought to give purely universal truths (which is indeed a partial truth).

But lurking in the midst of universal rational development was something of a time bomb—something that would kill its believed-to-be universal nature. And that was simply the next major stage of human growth and development, known variously as "pluralistic," "relativistic," "multicultural," or "postmodern." This stage was felt to be important because the "given-to-all" universal nature of rationality was felt to be too overbearing, too oppressive, and too pushy to be simply true and right for everybody. Surely there are important truths given by many cultures—various multicultural truths that might be true for me, too, even if I am not living in that culture? Different types of foods, of medicines, of health cares, and of raising and schooling children are some of the many different yet important truths that come from different multicultural sources.

And that very soon led (after the introduction of the pluralistic stage in the 1960s) to what would become known as a "post-truth" culture. "There are no universal truths" would become the motto of what was soon called "postmodernism" (post-objective, post-universal, post-truth culture). From that point on, you had to say, "Well, from this particular perspective, it seems true that . . ." Advocates of this postmodern approach even went so far as to claim that mathematical truths were no longer universally true. Welcome to the Age of Unreason.

And this is deeply ironic, because the whole point about developmental stages is that they literally include the previous stage but also go beyond it, bringing something new to it—they *"transcend and include"* their predecessor. So just as an atom transcends and includes protons and neutrons in its nucleus, and a molecule literally transcends and includes various atoms in itself, and a living cell transcends and literally includes all of its molecules, so a plant and an animal transcend and include their multicellular components. Likewise, the same thing occurs with a single letter and a word, a word and a sentence, a sentence and a paragraph, and a paragraph and a whole book or magazine article. A brilliant theorist named Arthur Koestler actually invented a word for such entities; he called them "holons." And according to Koestler, everything in the universe, except for "heaps" (like a heap of garbage without structure or inherent form), is a holon. It is itself composed of wholes, and it is also usually a part of a larger whole. This, incidentally, is why the human stages of development get larger and larger. They are holons—wholes composed of other wholes, which necessarily get bigger and bigger as they grow.

Remember when I said that the motto of the pluralistic postmodern stage of development was "there are no universal truths"? That seems to leave out rational truths altogether, yes? Well, that statement in itself actually *includes* a rational universal truth—it is really saying that "It is universally true that there are no universal truths"—thus including a rational component. And note that it not only "includes" that rational component, it "transcends" it as well, or includes some additional (transcendental) material—namely, "there are not only universal truths, there are also multicultural truths, truths that, while not fully universally true, are still true in some culture or another, and thus are multicultural truths." Well, that's an important partial truth, which is why "irrational" postmodernism came to replace rational modernism in such a short period of time (from the first true inception of pluralistic relativism in the 1960s to its full embrace in the 1990s is not much more than thirty years, compared to the Rational Age itself, which lasted from around 1605 to 1960, around ten times longer).

Well, this pluralistic time bomb was exactly that. It is still the largest major level of development that most people in the West are at (around 30 percent, although the rational stage does sometimes reach over 40 percent). And it is still eating away at our rational foundations (which include individual personhood, rights, dignity, self-respect, civic duty, and civility itself). And each day gives us more and more evidence of the decay. Talk about *The War on the West*—is it ever! Douglas Murray agrees with much of my assessment of the causes of this War (he talks about the attack on individualism, self-respect and self-loathing, decline of civic duty and civility itself, and the loss of Christianity, among others). The one item he doesn't include is the developmental component in all of this. Like virtually all scholars in the West, he just assumes that things like magic beliefs and mythic gods were simply present at some point in the past, but how or why they got there, he's silent on. This is not his fault (Murray is a fabulous scholar!); but virtually every academic in the West fails to realize that the reason that we have magic and mythic elements in our past is because in our actual past there was a real time when we were indeed *at* exactly those stages of Magic and Mythic development, and they remain as potentials for us even today—right now—because each of those stages has been "transcended and included" in our very makeup. It's not that somebody who has a completely rational capacity simply regresses and reverts to an irrational childhood state; it's that this irrational childhood state (magic or mythic) is still an ongoing part and parcel of our very own present being. We simply have not outgrown them enough; they remain active aspects of our essential makeup.

And with the Boomer generation, these states became very active again. This is why the Boomers are known as the "Me generation"—they reactivated the narcissistic mythic components of their very own selves, making themselves their own mythic gods and goddesses. Hence, exactly the society-wide explosion of narcissism, self-promotion, self-aggrandizement coupled with self-depression (when your inner god gets upset with you, that upset comes in mythically huge proportions), social fragmentation (no universally binding truths), and social polarization (just a lot of polar opposites existing everywhere, and as with all opposites, only one of them can be true at a time—pleasure vs. pain, good vs. evil, happy vs. sad, up vs. down—so again there is nothing universal to tie anything together). All of these problems came bursting onto the scene at about the same time, and all have remained to this day, tied together by the developmental stage that produced them, and that continues to bind them together—this pluralistic, relativistic, polarized, fragmented stage of human growth and development.

So is there a genuine way out of this mess? The response is, hopefully, yes there is. Since there is one, major, fundamental cause underlying all of this—namely, an active fixation to the multicultural, pluralistic, postmodern stage of development—there is an equally simple cure for the problem: namely, well, grow up and get over it!

That is perhaps a little easier said than done. But the cure is still fairly simple. We want to put into place, in our minds, a series of notions that will help us move beyond our fixation to this stage (and yes, on occasion, this would include ways to overcome any actual regression to this stage that we may encounter). That is the exact purpose of this book. We will, of course, first want to look specifically at development itself and get a real feel for its many stages, levels, and lines—and this, I promise you, is much more fun than it sounds. You'll be amazed at the number of things that you once believed (archaic, magic, mythic, rational, pluralistic, integral) and at how they all came voluntarily into existence in you at a particular time. You'll also get a sense of—a feel for—the various things that caused you to actually give up that particular belief and replace it with a completely different belief—amazing! And most importantly, since the next major stage beyond the pluralistic postmodern stage is the systemic integral stage, you will be introduced to a very simple and very easy to apply "integral model," or a model that claims (and millions of followers around the world agree) that it unites and integrates virtually all of the various human knowledge disciplines (Integral Business, Integral Art, Integral Spirituality, Integral Science, Integral Ethics, Integral Philosophy, Integral Psychology, and so on), all wrapped up and fully included in one simple, unifying, Integral Framework. As you understand how this framework operates (again, it's super easy), you will have a foolproof inner guide that directly counterbalances and counteracts any polarizing or fragmenting thoughts and ideas that your pluralistic stage might send your way, thus curing this problem more or less permanently in yourself.

What you will also find in this book is a unified political theory, which means pretty much what it sounds like. In the roughly six or so years since I first wrote this book, almost every prediction it made about the political landscape has come true, sometimes in an even more intensified fashion. It's been reported that even the predictions in two of Douglas Murray's books (which I mentioned paralleled my points rather exactly)—*The Strange Death of Europe* and *The Madness of Crowds*—came to be true so quickly that before they went to press he had to go through and revise the books to catch up with current events. There is some of that in this book. The modernist and the postmodernist Left and Right have continued to push things forward in this regard, and the aware reader will notice such happenings as January 6, Ukraine, Israel/Gaza, the rightward lurch in Europe, the upcoming presidential elections, and China/Taiwan. You will see how all of these events are brought together under one roof with the Integral Political Theory presented herein.

Well, shall we see?

Ken Wilber
November 2023
Denver, CO

A Note to the Reader

The election of Donald Trump as the forty-fifth president of the United States came as something of a complete surprise and, for many, a staggering shock. The responses to this surprise, from virtually all colors of the political spectrum, tended to be extreme, vocal, and intense. The Left seemed to overflow with an alarm that quickly turned to anger, vociferous regret, and even sharp hatred, which altogether drove—and continues to drive—hundreds of demonstrations, almost daily, around the country. The Right sat back with smug grins and not-so-veiled threats of "Things are gonna totally change!" and "Now we'll get even!"—threats that, indeed, Trump seems to have been acting on since day one in office.

In all of this, the more I listened to both sides, and read the voluminous outpouring of articles, essays, posts, and publications by all sides—purporting to tell us why this actually happened, what it really means, and what we should do about it—the less satisfied I became with what I heard. Although I agreed with numerous points raised by both sides, it seemed to me that virtually everybody was missing what is perhaps the single most central issue and crucial item for truly understanding what happened, why it did, and what it means. Truly, the core issue seems to have breezed over pretty much everybody's head.

And worse, in missing this central issue, the commentators had missed the crucial types of action that are necessary to redress the problem—that is, what responses would be most appropriate. But one thing has been clear: a country in which 50 percent of the population flat out hates the other 50 percent is not a country that can move forward with any sort of grace, dignity, and integrity. And that is exactly where the United States of America finds itself right now.

So I wrote an extended essay/short book on the topic, which you now are reading. I posted it at several online outlets, and it caused a rather immediate sensation, going a bit semi-viral. I'm an author and teacher by profession, so when a good number of people recommended I publish this piece, I spoke with my publisher. We decided to bring it out as a book immediately (and, for future reference to the exact historical location of the points the book makes, it was written, in its final form, around three months post-inauguration). Let me make a few very quick comments about it here.

First, this is not an attempt to give an overall analysis of all the factors that contributed to putting Donald Trump in office. Rather, although this presentation mentions many (or perhaps even most) of the other factors that were involved, it deliberately focuses on the one single—and, I believe, clearly most pertinent—issue that was responsible for this result, and it does so especially because, as I noted, this issue seems to have been completely overlooked by virtually all commentators of every stripe. For a full account of the Trump presidency, this factor needs to be included in a comprehensive analysis of all the other factors that are at play here. Still, this factor is indeed central (both for the major cause, and hence for the most appropriate courses of action in response).

Second, although my profession is indeed as a scholar (some twenty-three books in up to twenty-five foreign languages), this short book is not offered as a scholarly production. This is not an academic presentation; it's much more like an op-ed piece in a national newspaper. I have intentionally not included scholarly references for any of my quotes, sources, or facts; I want this to be an easy, straightforward presentation unencumbered by bulky academic apparatus. If interested, this data can always be Googled. If you do so, keep in mind what is actually involved in that search process—and exactly what that means is something that will become very clear as you read further.

Third, you will note that throughout this piece there are occasional references to things like "Integral Theory" or "Integral Metatheory," "AQAL," "Lower-Right quadrant," and such. These are simply technical terms from a general philosophical perspective, called "Integral," that I believe has much merit; indeed, the basic viewpoint of this piece is the Integral perspective. But if you're not interested in that type of thing, or at least don't want a dose of it right now, by all means simply ignore these terms when they occasionally appear; I have included them mostly for students. If you happen to find them intriguing, by all means, please pick up virtually any of my books (perhaps starting with *A Brief History of Everything* or *The Integral Vision*) to learn more about Integral Theory. All that needs to be said for now is that it is an orientation that has attempted to integrate most of the various branches of human knowledge—including premodern, modern, and postmodern approaches—and thus, if nothing else, this viewpoint definitely tends to be very inclusive and comprehensive. In short, you will find the discussion in the following pages to be very open-minded. But apart from that, there is truly no reason to be bothered or irritated by these occasional technical terms; by all means, simply ignore them.

Finally, this book is presented in three parts: An Overview, The Territory, and The Immediate Future. Chapter 2 in the Overview is a very short, very simple introduction to an extremely important, but rarely known, discipline and field of human knowledge. This field involves one of the most fundamental and truly profound aspects of human growth and development, but one that is almost always overlooked or ignored when we approach any of the major problems and issues confronting humanity today —an ignorance that I believe we pay for dearly. My colleagues and

I stumbled upon this incredible treasure during our worldwide search for all the important knowledge fields to be covered by Integral Metatheory, and its stunning importance immediately hit all of us right between the eyes, along with the shock of not having been introduced to it earlier (again, it is very well documented but very little known). You'll see exactly what this discipline is, get a quick (and very easy) introduction to it, and then see why it is so crucial to understanding the whole Trump phenomenon. I think you will enjoy this section, actually, and find that it offers a profoundly useful tool with which to approach virtually any area or problem in your life. Most of the people who learn about this evidence-based discipline claim that it totally changes the way that they look at the world, and it does so because it touches an area of being human that is as profound as profound can get. I hope you will agree—and enjoy!

Thank you, then, for joining me in this process of exploring one of the most significant historical events of our time, the repercussions of which will no doubt be staggering—not only for this country but for the entire world. And this exploration is also an *adventure* because it involves looking at a centrally core process of being human that happens to be operating in you as well, right now—an interior process that you will be directly introduced to in the following pages. This is a political analysis that is also a process of self-discovery, and that eye-opening possibility is what I truly hope you will take away from this book.

PART ONE

An Overview

1 : Self-Correction at the Leading-Edge

On balance, the response to the recent election of Donald Trump as the next president of the United States has been extreme, visceral, and loudly vocal, on all sides. The supporters of Trump have often been nasty and mean in their triumphal attitude, voicing "I told you so!" and "This finally serves you right!" as they gloat over their unexpected but, they feel, totally righteous and justified win. The anti-Trump side has been, if possible, even more vocal, with people tearfully telling of how they threw up, screamed, spent endlessly sleepless nights, and all but gave up on democracy and any sort of idealism at all (many had promised to leave the country should Trump win), finding his election to be a victory of hatred, racism, sexism, xenophobia, and all-round bad taste—and then, usually, vowing to continue "the fight" and urging their fellow Americans to fight with them, to never give up.

Both sides, in my opinion, are caught in too narrow a view. There is a bigger picture operating here, and I'd like to outline what that might possibly be. I've never heard this particular view I'm about to describe be expressed by anybody, but I believe it represents a larger, more integral view, and as such can be quite illuminating—and liberating. The pain and suffering that both sides feel is, I believe, the result of identifying with a much too narrow view, and a more expansive stance offers genuine release, while still allowing one to work on whatever side one wishes.

Every now and then, evolution itself has to adjust course in light of new information on how its path is unfolding, and it starts (apparently spontaneously but actually with this deeper morphic field operating) by making various moves that are, in effect, *self-correcting* evolutionary realignments. The leading-edge of cultural evolution is today—and has been for four or five decades—the green wave. ("Green" refers to the basic stage of human growth and development known to various developmental models as "pluralistic," "postmodern," "relativistic," "individualistic," "self-actualization," "diversity," "inclusion," "human-bond," "multicultural," and so on, and generically referred to as "postmodern." This is an area that I will clearly and simply outline in the next chapter. Right now, merely note that the large number of different names that I just listed for this item is an indication of how widespread the expert consensus is concerning it. For the moment, you can just remember it as "postmodern"; it joins "modern" and "traditional" as the three most populous value systems in this country. The confrontational and quite heated battles between them is known widely as "the culture wars," as we will continue to see.)

The primary purpose of the leading-edge of evolution—in today's case, the green, postmodern wave—is to be just that: a LEADING edge of evolutionary unfolding, what Maslow called a "growing tip," which seeks out the most appropriate, most complex, most inclusive, and most conscious forms that are possible at that particular time and point of evolution, pointing to new, novel, creative, and adaptive areas for the future to unfold into.

Beginning in the 1960s, green first began to emerge as a major cultural force, and it soon bypassed orange (which was the previous leading-edge stage, known in various models as "rational," "reason," "formal operational," "achievement," "conscientious," "accomplishment," "merit," "profit," "self-esteem," "self-authoring," "excellence," and "progress"—in short, "modern" in contrast to green's "postmodern") as the dominant leading-edge. Green started with a series of by-and-large healthy and very appropriate (and evolutionarily positive) forms: the massive civil rights movement, the worldwide environmental movement and drives for sustainability in business, the rise of personal and professional feminism, anti-hate-crime legislation, a heightened sensitivity to any and all forms of social oppression of virtually any minority, and—centrally—both the understanding of the crucial role of "context" in any knowledge claims and the desire to be as "inclusive" as possible. The entire revolution of the sixties was driven primarily by this stage of development—in 1959, 3 percent of the population was at green; in 1979, close to 20 percent of the population was—and these events truly and irrevocably changed the world. The Beatles (otherwise sacrosanct in my view) summarized the whole move (and movement) with one of their songs: "All You Need Is Love." (Total inclusion rules!)

But as the decades unfolded, green increasingly began veering into extreme, maladroit, dysfunctional, even clearly unhealthy forms. Its broad-minded pluralism slipped into a rampant and runaway relativism (collapsing into nihilism), as the notion that all truth is contextualized (or gains meaning from its cultural context) slid into the notion that there is no real universal truth at all, only shifting cultural interpretations (which eventually slid into a widespread narcissism). Central notions (which began as important "true but partial" concepts, but collapsed into extreme and deeply self-contradictory views) included the ideas that all knowledge is, in part, a social construction; all knowledge is context-bound; there are no privileged perspectives; what passes for "truth" is a cultural fashion, and is almost always advanced by one oppressive force or another (racism, sexism, Eurocentrism, patriarchy, capitalism, consumerism, greed, environmental exploitation); each and every human being, often including animals, is utterly, absolutely unique, and absolutely of equal value (egalitarianism). If there were one line that summarizes the message of virtually all of the truly prominent postmodern writers (Jacques Derrida, Michel Foucault, Jean-François Lyotard, Pierre Bourdieu, Jacques Lacan, Paul de Man, Stanley Fish, etc.), it is that "there is no truth." Truth, rather, was a social construction, and what anybody actually called "truth" was simply what some culture somewhere had managed to convince its members was truth; but there was no actually existing, given, real thing called "truth" that is simply sitting around awaiting discovery, any more than there is a single universally correct hem length that it is clothes designers' job to discover.

Even science itself was held to be no more true than poetry. (Seriously.) There simply was no difference between fact and fiction, news and novels, data and fantasies. In short, there was "no truth" anywhere.

So it ended up that, to the general postmodernist perspective, all knowledge is culturally bound; there is no universally valid perspective, therefore all knowledge is based on a mere interpretation announced from a privileged (therefore oppressive) perspective; knowledge is not given but is constructed (created, built, fabricated); there is nothing but history, and therefore what any culture might take as "true" today will dramatically shift tomorrow (What ever happened to the "seven deadly sins"? Half of them are clear virtues today.); there is no universal moral framework—what's true for you is true for you, and what's true for me is true for me—and neither of those claims can be challenged on any grounds that do not amount to oppression; the same is true for value—no value is superior to another (another version of egalitarianism)—and if any truth or value is claimed to be universal, or claimed to be true and valuable for all, the claim is actually nothing but disguised power, because it is simply an attempt to force all people everywhere to adopt the same truth and values of the promoter (with the ultimate aim of enslavement and oppression). It is therefore the job of every individual to fight all of the authoritarian truths handed to them from yesterday and to be totally, radically autonomous (as well as to not entertain any truths that could or should be forced on anybody else, to allow everybody their own radical autonomy as well—in short, to not entertain anything called "truth" at all, which now was seen as always being a power-grab).

Put bluntly, since everything handed to us by yesterday is not a real and enduring truth, just a fabricated fashion of history, it is our job to accept none of it, and instead only strive for a total, self-created, self-initiated autonomy (which very soon became indistinguishable from "Nobody interferes with my narcissism!"). You simply *deconstruct* every single truth and value you find (an approach that indeed rapidly slid into nihilism and, again, its tag-team member from postmodern hell, narcissism). In short, the aperspectival madness of "there is no truth" left nothing but nihilism and narcissism for motivating forces.

The catch-22 here was that postmodernism itself did not actually believe a single one of those ideas. That is, the postmodernists themselves violated their own tenets constantly in their own writings, and they did so consistently and often. Critics (from Jürgen Habermas to Karl Otto-Apel to Charles Taylor) would soon jump all over them for committing the so-called "performative contradiction," which is a major self-contradiction because you yourself are doing what you say either cannot or should not be done. For postmodernists, all knowledge is non-universal, contextual, constructivist, interpretive—found only in a given culture, at a given historical time, in a particular geopolitical location. Unfortunately, the postmodernists aggressively maintained that every one of their summary statements given in the previous paragraph were true for all people, in all places, at all times—no exceptions. Their entire theory itself is a very Big Picture about why all Big Pictures are wrong, a very extensive metanarrative about why all metanarratives are oppressive. They most definitely and strongly believed that it is universally true that there is no universal truth. They believed all knowledge is context-bound except for *that* knowledge, which is always and everywhere trans-contextually true. They believed all knowledge is interpretive, except for theirs, which is solidly given and accurately describes conditions everywhere. They believed their view itself is utterly superior in a world where they also believed absolutely nothing is superior. Oops.

Over two decades ago, in the book *Sex, Ecology, Spirituality*, I summarized this postmodern disaster with the term "aperspectival madness," because the belief that there is no truth—that no perspective has universal validity (the "aperspectival" part)—when pushed to extremes, as postmodernism was about to do, results in massive self-contradictions and ultimate incoherency (the "madness" part). And when aperspectival madness ("no truth") infects the leading-edge of evolution, evolution's capacity for self-direction and self-organization is bound to collapse.

It's widely acknowledged that postmodernism as a philosophy is now dead, and books written about "What comes next?" are starting to appear everywhere (with no clear winner yet, but the trend is toward more evolutionary and more systemic—more integral—views). But in academia and the universities, it is a long, slow death, and most teachers in the humanities still teach some version of postmodernism and its aperspectival madness even if they have many deep doubts themselves.) It's telling that virtually every major developmental model in existence contains, beyond the stage generally known as "pluralistic" or "postmodern," at least a stage or two variously called "integrated," "systemic," "integral," or some such, all of which overcome the limitations of a collapsed pluralism through a higher-level wholeness and unity, and thus return to a genuine "order out of chaos." Right now, only about 5 percent of the population is at any of these integral stages of development, but the evidence is that this is clearly where tomorrow's evolution eventually will go—if it can survive the present transition.

And thus postmodernism as a widespread leading-edge viewpoint slid into its extreme forms (e.g., not just that all knowledge is context-bound, but that all knowledge is *nothing but* shifting contexts; or not just that all knowledge is co-created with the knower and various intrinsic, subsisting features of the known, but that all knowledge is *nothing but* a fabricated social construction driven only by power). When it becomes not just that all individuals have the right to choose their own values (as long as they don't harm others), but that hence there is nothing universal in (or held in common by) any values at all, this leads straight to axiological nihilism: there are no believable, real values anywhere. And when all truth is a cultural fiction, then there simply is no truth at all—epistemic and ontic nihilism. And when there are no binding moral norms anywhere, there's only normative nihilism. Nihilism upon nihilism upon nihilism—"there was no depth anywhere, only surface, surface, surface." And finally, when there are no binding guidelines for individual behavior, the individual has only his or her own self-promoting wants and desires to answer to—in short, narcissism. And that is why the most influential postmodern elites ended up embracing, explicitly or implicitly, that tag team from postmodern hell: nihilism and narcissism—in short, aperspectival madness. The culture of post-truth.

There were many responses to this aperspectival madness— as a blanket, background, morphogenetic, leading-edge field, there were few areas in society that were not directly affected by it—and we will explore many of them in this overview. But the major driver behind all of them, the ultimate causative agent, was that the leading-edge of evolution itself had begun failing—badly, obviously, and often. When the leading-edge has no idea where it's going, then naturally it doesn't know where to go. When no direction is true (because there is no truth), then no direction can be favored, and thus no direction is taken; the process just comes to a screeching halt—it jams, it collapses.

Nihilism and narcissism are not traits that any leading-edge can actually operate with. And thus, if it's infected with them, it indeed simply ceases to functionally operate. Seeped in aperspectival madness, it stalls, and then begins a series of regressive moves, shifting back to a time and configuration when it was essentially operating adequately as a true leading-edge. This regression is one of the primary factors we see now operating worldwide, and the primary and central cause of all of this is a failure of the green leading-edge to be able to lead at all. Nihilism and narcissism bring evolution to a traffic-jam halt. This is a self-regulating and necessary move, as the evolutionary current itself steps back to reassess and reconfigure, a move that often includes various degrees of temporary regression, or the retracing of its footsteps, to find the point of beginning collapse and then reconfigure from there.

Evolutionary biologists in general tend to deny any sort of directedness or telic drives to evolution, seeing all of it as a random series of events and a blind natural selection. But this view is just a holdover from the reductionistic scientific materialism of the nineteenth century. It overlooks more current scientific concepts, starting with Ilya Prigogine's Nobel Prize–winning discoveries, that even insentient material systems have an *inherent* drive to self-organization. When physical systems get pushed "far from equilibrium," they escape this chaos by leaping into a higher-level state of organized order—as when water that is chaotically rushing down the drain suddenly leaps into a perfect downward-swirling whirlpool—referred to simply as "order out of chaos." If nonliving matter inherently possesses this drive to self-organization and order out of chaos, living systems certainly do—and that definitely includes evolution, a drive that philosophers often call "Eros," an inherent dynamic toward greater and greater wholeness, unity, complexity, and consciousness.

But this "order out of chaos" is exactly what the green leading-edge began failing to do. If anything, it was producing "more chaos out of chaos." It had no idea of what true order was to begin with; all such "metanarratives" were completely and aggressively deconstructed. Because nothing was true at all, there could be no true order, either, and hence no preferable direction forward. And so, as the leading-edge of evolution collapsed in a performative contradiction—lost in aperspectival madness—evolution itself temporarily slammed shut, and began various moves, including a regressive stepping back and searching for a sturdier point where a true self-organizing process could be set in motion once again. What previous stages are available for this regression? To answer this question, we need a brief summary of the overall developmental spectrum to date. The following overview is the result of a meta-analysis of over a hundred different developmental models and gives the most common features of all of them (see Wilber *Integral Psychology*). (Those familiar with Integral Metatheory can fast-forward through this or read it as a refresher. Those new to the concept can take it as a short introduction to one of the most profound and enduring discoveries of the twentieth century, accepted by experts everywhere who have fully studied the enormous amount of evidence that supports this idea.) As you read, you might note that these stages of development are available to you as well, and are operating in you right now. This is not just an academic exploration; it is a real process of self-discovery.

Let's see . . .

2 : That Ever-Expanding Stairway

The earliest stages of human development are together known as "egocentric" because they cannot yet take the role of other or clearly see the world through somebody else's eyes, or "walk a mile in my shoes." The earliest human societies (and here we are talking about the actual original indigenous populations, close to a half-million years ago, and not any indigenous population the way that it exists in today's world, where it has continued to evolve) were tribal (and tribally egocentric), with an ecological carrying capacity of around forty people. The thinking was usually imbued with fantasy (or "preoperational cognition"), and is often, as with Jean Gebser, called "magic" (as in voodoo, where if you make a doll representing a real person and stick a pin in the doll, the real person is "magically" hurt; if you perform a rain dance, nature is forced to rain).

When tribes ran into each other (which in many places originally was rare), it wasn't clear how they should interact, since the major form of relationship that was clearly understood was blood or kinship relations, and of course the tribes weren't related; often there was instead war or the taking of the other tribe as slaves (about 15 percent of original tribes had slavery); and as recent scholarship has demonstrated, debunking the popular highly romantic views, warfare was quite common.

(Keep in mind that as we describe these general stages of evolutionary development, this is a considerably condensed summary. There are hundreds or thousands—or more—of factors that

13

went into the emergence of each and every stage; each stage had limitations, but it also contributed something extremely positive to humanity's overall understanding of itself and the world, and subsequent humanity forgot those wisdoms at great cost—as, for example, many individuals seek to remind us today of the significant wisdom of indigenous cultures. The reason that earlier wisdoms need to be remembered is that in a healthy development, each stage "transcends but includes" its predecessor: it goes beyond or brings forth new and emergent truths not previously found, but it also needs to include and embrace the important previous truths themselves, at pain of developmental dysfunction and disharmony. Integral Metatheory explicitly focuses on these dozens and dozens of other factors, but right now we are following the genuine significance of just one of them—the levels of self-organization or the general stages of development itself. This is crucial because it is foundational in the values that any culture embraces, and also because, due to postmodernism's leading-edge influence over the past several decades, it is an item that has almost always been ignored or actively denied. This is a major imbalance that we need to redress to fully understand ourselves and our world; so this is what we're doing here. The unmistakable importance of these levels of evolutionary development will become clearer and clearer as we proceed.)

As evolutionary unfolding continued, through various intermediate stages, a major milestone was the emergence of a more complex cognitive capacity beyond magic, which developmental genius Jean Gebser called "mythic" (Jean Piaget's "concrete operational," or what James Fowler called a concrete "mythic-literal" stage). Here, with this general mythic stage, it was understood that human beings do not possess magic or miraculous power in any real sense (the more often that humans actually tried magic, the more often they found that it failed), but magic was too appealing to be totally surrendered all at once. Rather, it was transferred to a whole host of supernatural beings—gods and goddesses and elemental spirits—and those beings definitely could do magic. What's more, they would do it on your behalf if you knew how to correctly approach them—and thus magic power shifted from the self to various mythic god figures.

Hence began the transformation from the "magic" epoch to the great "mythic" epoch, starting around 10,000 B.C.E. Around the world, human beings everywhere began their incredibly intense search for the one true and correct way to approach, appease, and please these powerful mythic figures. It was truly a matter of life (possibly eternal) and death (possibly eternal), and it drove most forms of fundamentalist (or "mythic-literal") religion that almost everywhere arose at this time. (A Christian version of mythic-literal, for example, believes every word of the Bible is literally and absolutely true, the Word of God himself, so that Moses really did part the Red Sea, Christ really was born of a biological virgin, Lot's wife really was turned into a pillar of salt, and so on).

This stage, with its more complex cognitive capacity, also was able, for the first time, to clearly and extensively "take the role of other," and thus its primary identity could switch from the self or me-only to a group (or groups)—not just a self-contained tribe but a mega-tribe, an empire of dozens or even hundreds of tribes, a nation, a particular religion embracing millions, a political party, and so on—thus its identity expanded from *egocentric* to *ethnocentric* (based on a given race, color, sex, creed, and so forth). This stage, anchored in being identified with one special group as opposed to all others, has a very strong "us versus them" mentality. Usually, its own group is seen as—and deeply believed to be—special, select, the chosen people, even divine, identified by God himself (or the Goddess herself) as the one and only truly sanctified group in the world; all the others are infidels, apostates, nonbelievers, even demonic, and are usually bound for hell or unending reincarnations. And especially historically, when this ethnocentric stage first emerged, it was not a sin to kill infidels—in fact, as completely "other," infidels have no soul, and thus killing them is not only okay, it is often recommended, since it would return them to their one true God that they have so ignorantly denied in this life. The Crusades of the Middle Ages is a classic example of two fundamentalist mythic religions attempting to destroy the other in the name of the love of their specially held, one true God (as are many religiously inspired terrorist acts today—as we'll see, once a particular stage has emerged, it remains in existence and can be inhabited by any number of subsequent individuals).

Thus, the general attitude of this mythic-literal "us-versus-them" stage, by any number of different names, is jihad—holy war. The correct approach to a nonbeliever is—in order of increasing severity—to convince them, convert them, torture them, or kill them, but letting them alone in their mistaken beliefs is ungodly and to be avoided at all costs. The expanded capacity of this stage (including, in the shift from egocentric to ethnocentric awareness, the formation of very large super-tribes bound by a common belief, or a common set of rules and laws, or a common religion, and/or a common authority) led to many tribes being bound together into multi-group groups, often resulting in various massive empires of one form or another—and the age of classic traditional civilizations and the founding of the Great (Mythic) Religions was upon us. (This overall stage is referred to as "conformist," "conventional," "mythic," "mythic-literal," "belongingness," "law and order," "traditional," "socializing," "absolutistic," "ethnocentric," and in general is referred to as "amber.")

Slavery, war, and torture reached their zenith; some 80 to 90 percent of cultures, East and West, had slavery during this ethnocentric mythic age, as one favored group or mega-group had its way with other human beings. The Great Religions likewise promised salvation—but *only* if you believed their version of Spirit and adopted their one true path to "liberation"—they are, after all, the chosen people with the one and only true Reality. You cannot believe that Jesus is the one and only true way to heaven and also that Krishna is the one and only true way to heaven. Most of the Great (Mythic) Religions, as they were originally created, were inherently ethnocentric "us-versus-them."

(There are other functions that the great spiritual systems performed, and still perform. In addition to providing these large mythic belief systems, virtually all of them had "esoteric" or "inner" teachings, which were primarily involved not with changing belief systems but with changing states of consciousness, usually from what was said to be a fragmented, divided, suffering separate-self to a unified, enlightened, awakened awareness—a change known around the world as Enlightenment, Awakening, Metamorphosis, Satori, Moksha. But these changes in states of consciousness were not, by themselves, strong enough to change the structure of the common stages of development—magic, mythic, and so on—that were also occurring and that I am now summarizing. Thus, virtually every culture that had a "path of Liberation" to Enlightenment also had slavery—or was racist—and was patriarchal—or was sexist—among many other such ethnocentric traits, and Enlightenment wasn't powerful enough to cure them of that. Further, these esoteric traditions, particularly in the West, were always much less common than the typical mythic belief-system approaches. Finally, the general stages that we are tracking now—from primal archaic to tribal magic to traditional mythic and eventually to modern rational to postmodern pluralistic to just-emerging integral—are stages that all human beings will grow through, if they continue to develop; the change-of-state Enlightenment practices, on the other hand, are something that a person almost always has to voluntarily engage in—they do not come automatically to everybody. Moreover, you can engage in these Enlightenment practices at virtually any of these stages of development. Thus, what most people take to be the "Great Religions" are the various major mythic systems that everywhere arose around the world at this time. If you do happen to be involved with one of the esoteric or inner paths of Liberation—such as Zen Buddhism, centering prayer of contemplative Christianity, Kabbalah of Judaism, Sufism of Islam, and so forth—realize that when I say "mythic religions," those are *not* what I'm talking about. And, by the way, good for you.)

This great "ethnocentric" stage began—in transitional forms, such as "magic-mythic" or red-stage "warrior" cultures—around 10,000 B.C.E., and the rise of the great mythic-membership or traditional civilizations themselves started around 3000 to 2000 B.C.E. and peaked around 1400 C.E. In today's world, every child is born at very early "archaic" or "magic" and egocentric stages, which dominate ages 1 to 3; transitions to magic-mythic for around ages 4 to 7; ethnocentric mythic proper, with several substages, emerges for roughly ages 6 to 11; then the next major stage, the "rational," as we will see, emerges in today's world generally with adolescence; and there are yet higher stages to come, as we'll also see. However, the central point here is that adults can remain "stuck" or "fixated" at any of those earlier stages or substages. Indeed, research by Robert Kegan, of the Harvard Graduate School of Education, shows that 3 out of 5—or 60 percent—of Americans remain at ethnocentric or lower stages. If you think this *ethnocentric* stage—with its tendencies toward racism, sexism/patriarchy, misogyny, mega-tribal dominance, oppression, and fundamentalist religion—sounds a bit like hardcore far-Right Republicans, and that it starts to push into recognized Trump territory, you'd be right.

As evolution continued, there eventually emerged the widespread capacity to take a 3rd-person perspective (or the capacity to think in global, relatively objective and "universal" ways), and not just in the 2nd-person modes that mark the ethnocentric stages. This was a stunning advance—from "local" to "global"—and it began to appear in a culture-wide fashion with the Renaissance, then came to a fruition with the Enlightenment (which, like all stages, had positive and negative aspects; certainly the expansion of identity to a larger, more inclusive, less oppressive form was very positive). This "orange" stage marked the emergence of the period generally known as "modernity" (just as the previous mythic stage is known as "traditional"—again, we are tracing the three most populous value systems in this country—the traditional, the modern, and the postmodern—and seeing how each of them, in addition to many other factors, is also connected directly to a particular and very real stage of human development).

Among many other things, the emergence of orange meant the explosion onto the scene of what would become known as the "modern sciences": modern chemistry, modern physics, modern astronomy, modern biology, modern geology, and so forth. All in all, those sciences would add around a stunning three decades to the average person's lifespan worldwide, generate a global free market economy, bolster the birth of the nation-state, invent everything from automobiles to airplanes to skyscrapers, end most infectious diseases that had regularly killed half the population everywhere, and plop a person on the moon.

This evolutionary stage also meant that identity could expand from *ethnocentric* ("my special group" identity) to *worldcentric* (or "all-groups" or "all-humans" identity, which strived to treat all people—not just a *special* group but *all* people—fairly *regardless* of race, color, sex, or creed). This was a staggering shift in values— from ethnocentric group-centered to worldcentric all-humans-centered—and primarily for this reason, in a one-hundred-year time period (roughly 1770–1870), slavery was outlawed in every single worldcentric rational-modern society on the face of the planet—*the first time anywhere in human history that this had happened* (and that turns out to be a key fact to remember).

(This stage, which was the core of "modernity" and "modern values," is variously known as "reason," "rational," "formal operational," "achievement," "accomplishment," "merit," "progress," "strive drive," "self-authoring," "self-esteem," "conscientious," "scientific," "individualistic," and marks the beginning of the worldcentric stages—all of which Integral Metatheory generically calls "orange." Most Americans, even if their center of gravity remains at one of the earlier stages, reach the capacity to at least think from this orange stage. This worldcentric rational possibility emerges today usually during adolescence, though, again, whether someone actually embraces this stage or not as a central identity varies considerably. Most, although not all, people reach at least a mythic-ethnocentric stage of central-identity development—about 60 percent of the population, we saw—yet beyond that, things begin to diverge considerably, and so we have to actually state—that is, estimate—what stage a person's or a given group's average "center of gravity" is at. (Needless to say, whenever we speak of these types of stages or levels, it is meant in a very general sense, with multiple *lines* of development—such as cognitive, moral, emotional, aesthetic, and so on—each of which can span several different *levels* of development, so nobody is ever simply "at" a level. But the reason the concept is very useful is that most individuals—and most cultures and subcultures—tend to organize their thoughts and behavior around a "center of gravity" that, on average, focuses on a particular level simply because it is consistent and self-coherent to do so. Those average "centers of gravity" are what I'm referring to; again, their major importance will become clearer as we proceed.)

All other factors considered equal—and there are many—but from the developmental view alone, if the person's central identity remains at amber, ethnocentric, mythic-membership, they will evidence "traditional" values, since those are the inherent characteristics of that stage: fundamentalist religious beliefs, family values, highly patriotic, patriarchal, militaristic, conformist, usually homophobic, and often sexist. If they move on to the worldcentric orange rational stage, they will tend to display "modern" values: belief in science, progress, individual rights and freedom, merit, profit, incentive, and individualism. If they move on to the (still worldcentric) green pluralistic multicultural stage, they will usually embrace "postmodern" values: diversity, egalitarianism, radical equality, intense environmentalism, feminism, socialist-tending, sustainability. *The well-recognized battle between these three value systems is everywhere referred to as "the culture wars."* While the culture wars are widely recognized, what is not recognized almost anywhere is the developmental stages that are actually involved. And what is especially not recognized is that every major developmental model in existence has a yet-higher stage of development beyond all of those: known variously as "integrated," "systemic," "integral," "self-transforming," and such, it involves the unifying synthesis of all of those stages, and points to a genuine way beyond their inherent conflicts. We will, needless to say, be returning to this point, as it appears to be at least part of a major solution to all of the conflicts that otherwise are fated to plague humanity, as they globally now do. In other words, whatever solutions we offer for tomorrow—which will certainly include economic, technological, and political aspects—if they do not also *include these interior stages of consciousness development,* we will be doomed to repeat the same basic conflicts in an unending fashion: the same fundamental value wars will simply latch on to—and manifest through—whatever new economic, technological, and political structures that we create, and nothing will have fundamentally changed. Again, more on that as we proceed.

This orange rational-modern mode was the leading-edge of evolution until, as we noted at the beginning of this piece, the sixties, when the next-higher stage beyond the modern stage—namely, the "postmodern"—began to emerge on a significant scale. Indeed, the leading-edge of orange rational/business/scientific materialism was beginning to fail as an adequate leading-edge. It had reduced all knowledge to "it-knowledge," or objectivistic-materialistic-industrialized methodology, and of the profound trinity of "the Good, the True, and the Beautiful," it had thoroughly ditched the Good and the Beautiful (a catastrophe known as the "disenchantment of the world" and the "disqualified universe," as it reduced almost everything in existence to nothing but materialistic realities recognized by the science of sensorimotor physics). It had an inherent belief in worldcentric morality—or the idea that all people have intrinsic worth, regardless of race, color, sex, or creed, and that everybody deserves an equal opportunity economically and socially; worth in general can also be keyed to demonstrated merit—but it had been undercutting those beliefs consistently with its rabid tendency to positivism. And disastrously, it had created systems of social existence which, although they themselves embraced worldcentric morality, allowed ethnocentric and even egocentric stages to hijack them. And many scientific-capitalistic businesses began to do just that, with rampant greed and cut-throat competition through a "social Darwinism."

But the postmodern stage—Integral Metatheory's "green"—brought a 4th-person perspective into significant existence, which had the capacity to reflect on—and critically analyze—these 3rd-person "global" productions, and this is where green postmodernism (so named because it came after, and reflected on, the products of modernism) decided that this rational-modern mentality had, in too many ways, veered off course in destructive and counterproductive ways. And thus came the civil rights movement, the worldwide environmental movement (which became larger than any political party anywhere on the planet), emphasis on feelings and "coming from heart"—as opposed to rationality and "coming from the head" (since modern = rational, "postmodern" was often called "post-rational")—personal and professional feminism, and the sustainability movement (in business and elsewhere)—all of what I have called "the many gifts of green."

And yet, in the course of its development, driven largely (if often unknowingly) by arcane arguments in academia, the originally healthy pluralistic postmodernism increasingly became an extreme, overblown, self-contradictory, utterly dysfunctional relativism, which, we've seen, soon collapsed almost entirely into nihilism and narcissism. It's the nature of the leading-edge stage that its values, although they are only embraced directly by the stage itself, nonetheless tend to permeate or seep through the culture at large. For example, when the leading-edge was worldcentric orange rational—whose worldcentric or "all humans treated equally" values inherently included an anti-slavery stance—the Civil War was fought in America in order to end slavery, and over a million white boys (and blacks as well) died in the fight to end black enslavement, yet not much more than 10 percent of the population was actually at the orange stage. However, that value had seeped throughout the culture of the North, and many were willing to die for it (as many were in the French and American revolutions, which marked an orange democratic overthrow of amber ethnocentric monarchy/aristocracy). The battle here wasn't black versus white, it was orange versus amber. (This "orange versus amber" remains today the *central* issue in the race wars, as we'll see.)

But this "seepage" of leading-edge values will happen whether the permeating value happens to be really good or really goofy—and a really goofy seepage is what late, dysfunctional, unhealthy green gave the world culture: namely, "there is no truth." This post-truth attitude began seeping throughout the entire culture, and in many ways, it stuck—globally, profoundly, and in a way that caught orange (and healthy green itself) completely off guard (and they still have, basically, no idea where it came from and no idea how to fix it, thanks to a decapitated leading-edge that itself was the actual source of the problem).

We'll come back to our post-truth culture—and its multiple catastrophes—but right now, let me finish with the basic major milestones of human development to date, because although green is today's major leading-edge stage (represented by around 20 to 25 percent of the population), there is nonetheless a yet-higher stage, which I briefly mentioned, that has begun to emerge in an as-yet small number of individuals. Beginning two or three decades ago, developmental researchers began to notice the emergence of a stage that, in its actual contours, was very confusing. Each major stage to date has had a common characteristic: each one thought that its truth and values were the only real truth and values in existence—all the others were misguided, infantile, goofy, or just plain wrong. But this new stage had a radically new quality: it believed that all the previous stages had some sort of significance, that they all were important, and that they all must be included in any approach that hoped to be comprehensive, inclusive, and truly integrated. For this reason, it was usually called things like "integrated," "systemic," "integral," and so on, and it marked a staggeringly new and radically different type of evolutionary stage altogether, unique in the entire history of humanity. Clare Graves, a pioneering developmentalist, called it "cataclysmic" and a "monumental leap of meaning." As noted, around 5 percent of the population has reached this stage in our ongoing unfolding (I'll have more to say about that in a moment). Because of its radically new and unprecedented nature, it is often called "2nd tier" to distinguish it from all the previous stages to date, which altogether are called "1st tier." 2nd tier marks an absolutely unheard of and radically new direction in human evolution altogether, the likes of which humanity has simply never seen.

That is, put bluntly, 2nd tier changes absolutely everything.

3 : The Birth of a Post-Truth Culture

B ack to the post-truth culture that a collapsed green had left us with. The promoters of Brexit openly admitted that they had pushed ideas that they fully knew were not "true," but they did so "because there really are no facts," and what really counts is "that we truly believe this." (As one of them tellingly noted, "I've read my Lacan—it's whoever controls the narrative that counts," citing Jacques Lacan, a leading postmodernist.) In other words, narcissism is the deciding factor—what I *want* to be true *is* true in a post-truth culture. President Trump doesn't even try to hide this; he lies factually with gleeful abandon. Reporter Carl Bernstein, of Watergate fame, stated that "Trump lives and thrives in a fact-free environment. No president, including Richard Nixon, has been so ignorant of fact and disdains fact in the way this president-elect does." His campaign manager, Kellyanne Conway, said that this is not really lying, it is just "alternative facts" (to which one reporter responded, "'Alternative facts' means falsehoods"). But when there are no facts to begin with, nobody tells lies or falsehoods, just alternative, equally valuable facts.

While Trump was campaigning, there were newspapers that actually kept count of the number of factual lies he had spoken, day by day: "Yesterday, it was 17 lies. Today, it was 15 lies." The website Politifact posts such counts and concluded that approximately 50 percent of everything Trump claimed was not factually true (!). And yet polls consistently showed that people felt Trump was "more truthful" than Hillary Clinton (who, no matter how much of an atmosphere of "corruption" followed her, as many believed, she never set out explicitly and blatantly to lie, or certainly nowhere near as much as Trump). But people had already made the transition from "factual truth" to "what I say is truth," and Trump said his "truth" with much more conviction and passion than Hillary could muster—and thus in a no-truth culture, Trump was the "more truthful." In a culture of nihilism, in an atmosphere of aperspectival madness where there is no real truth, truth becomes whatever I most fervently desire—in a sea of nihilism, passionate narcissism is the key determinant.

Note that the Boomers—the children of the sixties—are often called "the Me generation" and the "culture of Narcissism." And, compared to previous generations, this tended to be very true. As Boomers themselves began taking over education in this country, they significantly began shifting it so that education emphasized, first and foremost, a movement not of "teaching truth"—because there is no truth—but instead of promoting "self-esteem." And what they discovered—as a *Time* magazine cover story reported—is that promoting self-esteem, without anchoring it in actual accomplishments, simply ends up increasing narcissism. (Again, in a sea of no-truth nihilism, narcissism is all that's left—what else *could* the Boomers promote?) And indeed, the recent graduating class of Boomer-taught kids scored higher on amounts of narcissism than any class *since testing began*—some 2 to 3 times higher than their Boomer "Me generation" parents! Hence, one wag suggested calling this the "Me-Me-Me generation." In any event, a narcissistic emphasis on "special me" had indeed seeped into the culture at large. Among many other items, we would see the emergence of the "selfie culture," which notoriously and easily altered, even Photoshopped, individual truth, and whose social media began promoting "pleasing lies" and "reassuring falsehoods" in echo chambers that never dared to challenge one's special self-promoting facts.

Meanwhile, the leading-edge green cultural elites—upper-level liberal government, virtually all university teachers (in the humanities), technology innovators, human services professionals, most in the media and entertainment, and most highly liberal thought leaders—continued to push into green pluralism/relativism—"what's true for you is true for you, and what's true for me is true for me"—all largely with intentions of pure gold, but shot through with an inherently self-contradictory stance with its profound limitations. (Thus, for example, the statement itself— "what's true for me is true for me, and what's true for you is true for you"—actually claims to be a superior truth that is not open to challenge, and you are not supposed to disagree with that statement and actually have your own different opinion. You're definitely not supposed to think that "what's true for me is true for me, and it also better be true for you, too," even though the statement itself claims you can. If *that's* your truth, you are definitely *not* allowed to have it, or I'll claim you're a fascist or some such, since you're trying to force *your* truth on me.) In addition to the problem of self-contradiction, there's the problem that, if all truth is just truth for me and a different truth for you, then there is no "truth for *us*"—or collective, cohering, unifying truths. Hence, in this atmosphere of aperspectival madness, the stage was set for massively fragmented culture, which the siloed boxes and echo chambers of social media were beginning to almost exclusively promote and enhance.

Now green itself is a worldcentric stage. Although it gets theoretically confused about anything being "worldcentric" (or "universal")—namely, it thinks that all such moves are oppressive and power-driven—we've seen that green postmodernism itself deeply believes that what it is saying is true for all people; it doesn't apply to just one group or another ("ethnocentric"), it applies to all groups, all humans ("worldcentric"). But under its own confusion of aperspectival madness, where you cannot criticize any particular value (since all are egalitarian) and all worldcentric or universal stances are aggressively denied, individuals are allowed to actively slide into, even regress to, ethnocentric stances. *And thus the postmodern-created online social media began regressing into decidedly ethnocentric-leaning groups.*

And this happened on the conservative and liberal sides alike. On the conservative side, it was led by "trolls," or truly nasty ethnocentric Web surfers who posted endless condemnations aimed at any minority or minority viewpoint, and who were genuinely mean-spirited and spewing enormous amounts of anger and hatred. Yet liberals as well gleefully joined the ethnocentric stampede. Having implicitly denied any worldcentric or universal truths, liberals simply began an obsessive search for ethnocentric after more ethnocentric after yet more ethnocentric. One of the results of this slide, among many, was "identity politics," where you actively and aggressively identify with (and define yourself solely as) just one race or class or sex or creed (or political orientation or religion or nationality, and so on)—exactly a slide from worldcentric to ethnocentric identity. And if you're not a member of an obvious minority identity, then you have no real voice in how this country should culturally move forward (whereas real weight would be given to, say, a transgendered, bipolar, female Muslim, which is ethnocentric to the fourth power). There's not a single thing wrong with any one of those minorities—and every reason they should be fairly and liberally embraced in a worldcentric stance. But if you listen to *only* decidedly ethnocentric-identified voices, then that evidences exactly the partiality and divisiveness you claim you're trying to overcome. This is a slide exacerbated by the fact that it is openly and vocally embraced with hyper-pride. (It's fine to be proud of one's race or sex or creed, as long as it is alongside other such types and not *instead of* them or *above* them or *superior* to them, which all too often is exactly where identity politics ends up.)

With no truth to slow it, this regression to ethnocentric— by liberals and conservatives alike—simply exploded all over the Web. The original intent of the Internet was for a global, free, unified humanity, unleashed from oppression, information ownership, power structures, and isolating trends in general. The Net was proclaimed a single grand "global brain," open to and actively embracing all. The problem is, if the brain was global (or a single infrastructure network), the minds using it were not. As Douglas Rushkoff has pointed out, the very nature of the digital environment itself tends toward either/or types of decisions (either 1 or 0, click here or click there, choose this or choose that). And the anonymity and personality-hiding nature of online exchange allowed and even fostered regressive tendencies of aggression, narcissism, hatred, and innumerable passionate ethnocentric beliefs (sexist, racist, xenophobic, zealous religious, bigoted political, those of trolls and identity politics), and with no "truth" available to challenge any of these moves, they exploded. The entire online experience collapsed from one of unity, open-natured expanse, and worldwide integration, into one of siloed, boxed, separatist, mean-spirited ethnocentric drives. And these poured out of our laptops and smartphones 24/7 and into the culture at large.

A NEW AND ALARMING LEGITIMATION CRISIS

The problem very quickly became what Integral Metatheory calls a "legitimation crisis," which it defines as a mismatch between Lower-Left, or cultural, beliefs and the Lower-Right systems, or actual background realities, such as the techno-economic base. ("Left" and "Right" do not here refer to political parties but simply to their location on a typical 4-quadrant chart: the "Left-Hand" quadrants represent invisible interior realities—such as those of morals, values, consciousness, and beliefs—and the "Right-Hand" quadrants refer to visible exterior realities—such as concrete techno-economic systems and environments. And a "legitimation crisis" is a profound conflict and mismatch between these two dimensions in any society.)

The cultural belief was that everybody is created equal, that all people have a perfect and equal right to full personal empowerment, that nobody is intrinsically superior to anybody else (beliefs that flourished with green). Yet the overwhelming reality was increasingly one of a stark and rapidly growing *inequality*—in terms of income and overall worth, property ownership, employment opportunity, healthcare access, and life satisfaction issues. The culture was constantly telling us one thing, and the realities of society were consistently failing to deliver it—the culture was lying. This was a deep and serious legitimation crisis: a culture that is consistently lying to its members simply cannot move forward for long. And if a culture has "no truth," it has no idea when it's lying—and thus it naturally lies as many times as it accidentally tells the truth; hence, faster than you can say "deconstruction," it's in the midst of a legitimation crisis.

When it came to the problems of unemployment and wealth inequality, leading-edge technology also was not helping. (Not to mention the fact that capital itself, as economist Thomas Piketty pointed out, was inherently biased toward favoring the rich and excluding the poor.) Technology had long moved into being the material-system correlate (in the Lower Right) of the cultural beliefs of the green stage (in the Lower Left). The green "Information Age" believed that all knowledge is equal, and it should be totally free and totally uncensored—it was common to say that the Net interprets censorship as a system failure and routes around it. But search engines did not prioritize knowledge in terms of truth, or goodness, or beauty, or inclusivity, or any depth, or any value system at all—not even a growth hierarchy of values or facts— just in terms of popularity and most use. Truth played no role in it. Facebook finally admitted that it posted many "fake news" stories on its platform, which many have claimed helped Trump to win. It did so simply because its algorithms weren't created to check for truth, just the user's narcissistic tendencies. And it is now faced, along with every other online news outlet, with the necessity of creating algorithms that detect—and bracket—"fake news" items, which is going to be much harder than imagined given a background of "no truth" to work from.

(Another reason that "fake news" will not be that easy to sort out has to do with the *partial* truth of postmodernism: all knowledge is context dependent. This partial truth is indeed true, and is fully incorporated into Integral Metatheory. But what this means is that, in addition to the phenomenological world of basic, sensorimotor facts, there are the very real worlds of red realities or facts, amber realities or facts, orange realities or facts, green realities or facts, and turquoise realities or facts. Thus, when it comes to something like Columbus's first voyage to the Americas, a sensorimotor fact is that it did indeed occur in 1492. That is true; that is indeed a fact—a sensorimotor or physical fact. But when it comes to the facts regarding things like, "Why did Columbus do this?" "What effect did it have on the natives?" and "What were the overall results?" each level of being and awareness has a different context, and a different co-construction, regarding those answers. Each of them will therefore give answers that reflect the "reality" or the "facts" of its level—and each of those levels or stages differs significantly. What you don't want to do with such a contextual field of facts is to deny truth or facts altogether, because that denies the realities that any and all levels are actually aware of—and that is the disaster we are examining now. When it comes to the further issue of, "So, given a growth hierarchy of different but real facts at each level, how exactly do you determine what is genuinely truth, or what facts are actually real?" it is, needless to say, a very complex issue for which I recommend Integral Metatheory, which approaches this topic precisely and very directly. We'll also return to this issue very briefly a little later on. For now we are dealing with the much more specific and simpler issue of what happens when truth itself, or facts altogether, are denied—and how the Net itself has fallen prey to this disastrous tendency of aperspectival madness. *That* is the issue here.)

In terms of searching, in a sea of aperspectival madness, not for truth or goodness or beauty—and especially bypassing "truth" entirely—and looking just for narcissistic popularity, Google itself has recently been slammed with exactly that charge of dismissing or distorting truth, and those screaming "J'accuse!" are rightly and massively alarmed.

Carole Cadwalladr, in a recent *Guardian* article, pointed out that Google's search algorithms reflect virtually nothing but the popularity of the most-responded-to sites for the search inquiry. There is nothing that checks whether any of the recommendations are actually true (or good or beautiful or unifying or integrating or any other value, and express only the aperspectival madness of "no truth to be favored"). Cadwalladr was particularly alarmed when she typed in "Are Jews . . . " and before she could finish, Google's search engines had provided the most likely responses, one of which was "Are Jews evil?" Curious, she hit that entry, and was taken to the authoritative Google page of the ten most common and popular answers, nine of which said, in effect, "Yes, definitely, Jews are evil."

Genuinely surprised—and disturbed—she states, "Google is knowledge. It's where you go to find things out. And evil Jews are just the start of it. There are also evil women. . . . This is what I type: 'a-r-e w-o-m-e-'. And Google offers me just two choices, the first of which is: 'Are women evil?' I press return. Yes, they are. *Every one of the 10 results 'confirms' that they are* [my emphasis], including the top one . . . , which is boxed out and highlighted: 'Every woman has some degree of prostitute in her. Every woman has a little evil in her. . . . Women don't love men, they love what they can do for them.'"

With her disbelief—and alarm—growing, Cadwalladr continues, "Next I type: 'a-r-e m-u-s-l-i-m-s'. And Google suggests I should ask: 'Are Muslims bad?' And here's what I find out: yes, they are. That's what the top result says and six of the others. . . . Google offers me two new searches and I go for the first, 'Islam is bad for society.' In the next list of suggestions, I'm offered: 'Islam must be destroyed.'"

Here's her response:

> Google *is* search. It's the verb, to Google. It's what we all do, all the time, whenever we want to know anything. We Google it. The site handles at least 63,000 searches a second, 5.5bn [billion] a day. Its mission as a company, the one-line overview that has informed the company since its foundation and is still the banner headline on its corporate website today, is to "organise the world's information and make it universally accessible and useful". It strives to give you the best, most relevant results. . . .
>
> Jews are evil. [Women are evil.] Muslims need to be eradicated. And Hitler? Do you want to know about Hitler? Let's Google it. "Was Hitler bad?" I type. And here's Google's top result: "10 Reasons Why Hitler Was One of the Good Guys". I click on the link: "He never wanted to kill any Jews"; "he cared about conditions for Jews in the work camps". . . . Eight out of the other 10 search results agree.

Google is most definitely not "organizing the world's information and making it universally accessible and useful." It is disorganizing the world's information in an atmosphere of aperspectival madness, taking "diversity" to such an extreme that all views have an egalitarian and perfectly equal claim to validity—if, and only if, each wannabe truth is backed with enough passionate narcissism and outrageously fervent belief to make it really popular. And Google makes its living by selling these post-truths and alternative facts. Lies don't come cheap; there's a hefty advertising fee to reach these groups—and the more passionate and intense and vigorous the vote rating, the higher the advertising rates. This is because these groups with similarly held beliefs—"All women are evil"—compose highly motivated markets for the products that the advertiser wants to promote, because these groups are what are called "lookalike audiences"—that is, they all look and think alike in an echo chamber, totally predisposed to agree with one post-truth or alternative fact, such as "all Muslims must be destroyed" or "all Jews are evil." These statements are not anything resembling real truth, but are the very passionately held ethnocentric prejudices passing for truth in a post-truth world gone slightly mad. And Google is doling these out to the world as fast as it humanly and robotically can, 63,000 times a second, 5.5 billion times a day.

(Due to serious protests, Google deliberately overrode its algorithm and manually, as it were, altered some of the above results—apparently not of its own volition, but in response to the very vocal protests. Does the removal of the many thousands of similar items also await protest, because they don't appear to be disappearing on their own? Google's Jigsaw company has created a program called Perspective, whose algorithm focuses on detecting "toxicity," or items that are likely to offend somebody and drive them out of a conversation. But this is still not truth-checking; it's just offensiveness-checking. Not the same thing. Truth just doesn't seem to register.)

No wonder reports keep showing up like the one called "The Miseducation of Dylann Roof" (a video presented by the Southern Poverty Law Center, SPLC). Dylann Roof was a very young man who, seemingly for no reason at all, randomly shot and killed nine African Americans while they were praying at the historic Emanuel Church in Charleston, South Carolina. (Not central to this particular presentation, but deeply notable for its radiant goodness, is the stunning and completely sincere compassion that most of these families displayed and expressed directly to the murderer—not hatred and revenge, but love and forgiveness—and as a galvanized, frozen-with-awe nation looked on, dry eyes hard to find, family member after family member looked directly at Roof and forgave him. There is surely a lesson in here for the time that we are discussing now, which has more than a small amount of its own hatred in play.)

Roof was raised in a by-all-accounts quite decent family, with no history of racism or racial hatred. As he tells the story in his online manifesto (written shortly before the deadly attack), he says that he heard of a lethal shooting between a black and a white man, the first time he had really noticed something like that, and so "more importantly this prompted me to type the words 'black on white crime' into Google, and I have never been the same since that day."

He has never been the same because the search engine kept driving him to site after site simmering with "facts" quite similar to "all Jews are evil" and "all Muslims should be destroyed"—"facts" about how violent African Americans are, how they are a "retrograde species" that "should be eliminated." The SPLC maintains that this misinformation itself was the basis for what drove Roof to his crimes, according to what Roof himself has said. Whatever we decide about that, it is definitely true, as the SPLC puts it, that "the truth got submerged."

Google explicitly counters these kinds of charges by claiming that "Google's algorithm takes into account how *trustworthy, reputable,* and *authoritative* the source is." But do the statements "All women are evil," "All Jews are evil," "All Muslims must be destroyed," and "African Americans are a retrograde species" (as one website told Dylan Roof when he searched "black on white crime")—does any one of those sound anywhere near "trustworthy," or "reputable," or "authoritative"? That's so deeply off the mark, how did Google even come to claim something like that? How could it be so dismissive of truth as to not even include it as selection criteria in its search algorithms? One answer: in a "post-truth" culture, truth has simply dropped off our list of genuinely valued and idealized items. And that is exactly how Google, Facebook, "fake news," "alternative facts"—all of those and more—have already become part of the disastrous, but to-be-expected, new morals for the new century. "Fake news" is the new news.

I'll finish with Cadwalladr's story—it has such an unsettling ending. Being genuinely concerned about, even disturbed by, her discoveries about Google's seemingly built-in lack of concern for truth, Cadwalladr contacted Danny Sullivan, founding editor of Search Engine Land (searchengineland.com). "[Sullivan has] been recommended to me by several academics as one of the most knowledgeable experts on search. Am I just being naive, I ask him? Should I have known this was out there? 'No, you're not being naive,' he says. 'This is awful. . . . Google is doing a horrible, horrible job of delivering answers here.' . . . He's surprised, too. . . . [H]e types 'are women' into his own computer. 'Good lord! That answer at the top. It's a featured result. It's called a 'direct answer.' This is supposed to be indisputable. It's Google's highest endorsement.' That every woman has some degree of prostitute in her? 'Yes. This is Google's algorithm going terribly wrong.'"

And it's going "terribly wrong" because today's leading-edge has virtually no idea of what "genuinely right" could possibly mean. The *Guardian* highlights the overall piece by pointing out that it doesn't apply just to Google, but also to Facebook and, indeed, the general Internet culture itself: "The Internet echo chamber satiates our appetite for pleasant lies and reassuring falsehoods and has become the defining challenge of the 21st century."

How could an item have become the "defining issue" of our century without virtually every university in the world spewing out postmodern poststructuralist nostrums centering on the idea that "truth" itself is the single greatest oppressive force in the history of humankind? (Seriously.) Originated by the green leading-edge in academia, this aperspectival madness of "no truth" leapt out of the universities, and morphed into an enormous variety of different forms—from direct "no truth" claims, to rabid egalitarianism, to excessive censoring of free speech and unhampered knowledge acquisition, to extreme political correctness (that forced the best comedians to refuse to perform at colleges anymore, since the audiences "lacked all sense of humor": you're allowed to laugh at nothing in a "no value is better" world—even though that value itself was held to be better), to far-left political agendas that in effect "equalized poverty," to egalitarian "no judgment" attitudes that refused to see any "higher" or "better" views at all (even though its own view was judged "higher" and "better" than all the others), to modes of entertainment that everywhere eulogized egalitarian flatland, to a denial of all growth hierarchies by confusing them with dominator hierarchies (which effectively crushed all routes to actual growth in any systems anywhere), to the media's sense of egalitarian "fairness" that ended up trying to give equal time to every possible, no matter how factually idiotic, alternative viewpoint (such as Holocaust deniers), to echo-chambered social media where "pleasant lies" and "reassuring falsehoods" were the standard currency (and which were educating kids daily on how to lie and fake the truth socially). It saturated the leading-edge of evolution itself, throwing it into a performative contradiction and a widespread, explicit or implicit, aperspectival madness that was soon driven by nihilism and narcissism and a whole post-truth culture, which even invaded the Internet and bent it profoundly. That brokenness perfused the entire information grid of the overall culture itself—exactly the type of profound and extensive impact you expect a leading-edge (healthy or unhealthy) to have.

It has indeed become the defining issue of our century, because not a single other issue can be directly and effectively addressed if there is no compass point of accessible truth to guide action in the first place. In this catastrophic wasteland, the world is now suspended.

PART TWO

The Territory

4 : No Truth and No Jobs: "Ressentiment"

The essentially green Information Age began, with its artificial intelligence (AI), to mimic how human beings think, and as such, it began producing robots that could perform many of the types of work that human beings usually did. These started out as simple manual-labor jobs—inventory storage, online orders, welding, assembly-line work, and such—but have increasingly been moving into more and more complex jobs, including most financial investing, payroll accounting, news copy, middle management tasks, and—soon—truck driving and all driving jobs, as well as medical diagnoses and nursing chores, even surgeries. One think tank estimated that 50 percent of present-day jobs will be taken by robots by the year 2050, and another even estimated 47 percent of jobs by as soon as 2020. That's the destruction of fully *half* of today's jobs—and there's no AI analyst alive that doesn't think that's just the beginning.

In the meantime, over the past three to four decades, the median income has remained the same, whereas the average income has significantly increased—which means, those individuals at the top of the pay scale (the so-called "1 percent") are making a fortune, while most of the rest of the population stagnates or actually loses ground. This is another abject failure of the leading-edge to do what any leading-edge is supposed to do, which is to effectively lead, not stagnate, a culture.

It looks like, as AI continues its inexorable advance, that

within perhaps one hundred years, virtually all human work will be robotized. This is actually a terrific, near utopian result. After all, work has been taken as an inevitable curse on humans ever since day one. It has always been viewed as the necessary evil that all humans are egregiously condemned to suffer—and hence, in many cases, humans have created things like slavery, or the attempt to outsource the evil task. And now it looks like technology will finally end that evil once and for all. But the period of actually getting to that point, where virtually 100 percent of the population is free of work, will be a time of enormous pain for billions of human beings, as countless people lose their jobs with nothing to support them. This is why Silicon Valley—which is, whether it admits it or not, working as fast as it can to put as many people out of work as soon as possible—takes it as a matter of uncontested faith that something like a guaranteed basic income for everybody will soon be put in place, which is almost certainly necessary. (All things considered equal, I definitely agree with it.)

In the meantime, the leading-edge of both green "no-truth" and techno-economic "no-job" had created a seething, quietly furious, and enormously large amount of what Nietzsche called "ressentiment," which is French for *resentment*. Nietzsche meant it specifically for the type of nasty, angry, and mean-spirited attitude that tends to go with "egalitarian" beliefs (because in reality, there are almost always "greater" and "lesser" realities—not everything is or can be merely "equal"—and green resents this mightily, and often responds with a nasty and vindictive attitude, which Integral theorists call "the mean green meme"). But the notion of "ressentiment" applies in general to the resentment that began to increasingly grow, stemming from the severe legitimation crisis that had begun to soak the culture (which itself was, indeed, due primarily to a broken green). Everywhere you are told that you are fully equal and deserve immediate and complete empowerment, yet everywhere are denied the means to actually achieve it. You suffocate, you suffer, and you get very, very mad.

Leading-edge green, in the meantime, had taken to undoing what looked like oppression anywhere it could find it, and with regard to virtually any minority. This goal is undoubtedly noble and very worthwhile, but it was taken—by a zealous and now dysfunctional green—to absurd extremes, in a way that its opponents derisively called "political correctness." This has become such a hot button that the political divide has now become between those who see themselves as social justice advocates—pursuing oppression anywhere, looking for "triggers," "micro-aggressions," and creating "safe spaces"—versus those who see themselves as against an out-of-control political correctness, and standing behind First Amendment free speech and against what they see as hyper-sensitive liberal do-gooders who are destroying the very capacity for the free pursuit of ideas and open knowledge. (My stance is that both of them are partially true, as I'll explain.)

But the extremes of political correctness really did become extreme. There was a full-fledged sit-in at UCLA because a professor had actually corrected the spelling and grammar on a graduate-level exam—the students angrily claimed it created an "atmosphere of fear." Well, certainly when there is no truth, then forcing your version of spelling on somebody is an oppressive power drive. (Apparently, "the spelling that's true for you is true for you, and the spelling that's true for me is true for me.") In one feminist meeting, after the first speaker was given a round of applause, one woman reported that the applause gave her anxiety, and so the group voted to stop applauding for the rest of the conference. These are simply cases of a person's hyper-sensitivity being taken to extremes, and instead of seeing the person as themselves perhaps suffering from an emotional problem, they are labeled "victim," and then it's everybody else's job to cater to their narcissistic whims. Again, nihilism and narcissism have no place in the leading-edge (if it is to function at all).

It got so bad on college campuses that many of the most gifted comedians simply stopped doing campus shows entirely, including true geniuses like Chris Rock (probably the funniest person in America) and Jerry Seinfeld (the most successful TV comedian in history). They said that college campuses have "no sense of humor at all"—you can make fun of virtually nothing (given a hyper-sensitive egalitarianism)—and so they were not going to do it anymore. When gifted comedians can no longer even comment on a situation, something has gone very, very wrong. (The repression of humor is also one of the textbook moves of all authoritarian regimes, but this is coming from liberals, not conservatives!—coming, that is, from a broken green continuing its regression to ersatz ethnocentric absolutisms: "no laughing!") Extreme political correctness is simply aperspectival madness gone emotionally berserk.

So we've seen just a few of the ways that the green leading-edge of cultural evolution itself became derailed, became significantly dysfunctional and unhealthy, and was blindsided by a performative contradiction resulting in an epidemic aperspectival madness. And under such circumstances, evolution finds that it's necessary to take certain self-correcting moves. These moves will not obviously appear to be necessary correctives—they might indeed appear alarming. But the only thing more alarming would be for evolution to try and move forward on the basis of an already badly broken leading-edge. The disasters would simply increase. Green, as a leading-edge, had collapsed, and evolution itself had no choice but to take up a broadly "anti-green" atmosphere as it tried to self-correct the damage.

And the one thing that was true of Donald Trump—more than any other single characteristic that defined him (more than his sexism, more than his racism, more than his xenophobia)—is that every word out of his mouth was anti-green.

STAGES OF DEVELOPMENT AND POLITICAL PARTIES
Now this means that Trump's anti-green rhetoric could have resonated with and activated, in general, one (or more) of the

three main pre-green stages: it could have activated orange world-centric (achievement, merit, progress, excellence, profit); it could have activated amber ethnocentric (racist, sexist, xenophobic, anti-immigrant, hyper-terrorist-sensitive, homophobic, hyper-bolic patriotic); or it could have activated red egocentric (pre-conventional, self-serving, self-promoting, narcissistic).

Now before we discuss which of those it actually did activate, let's trace how the main political parties line up in terms of those major stages of human development. There are numerous different variables that go into whether one is conservative/traditional or liberal/progressive (and these span the entire AQAL matrix). But in the most simplistic terms (and focusing just on levels), the original liberal party was born with the Western Enlightenment, when the "Left" was named simply for the fact that its members sat in the left-hand seats in the French parliament. What it represented—and what made it a basically new political movement in history—was the newly emergent orange, rational, worldcentric, meritocratic, post-mythic, post-religious, pro-science, progressive level of development. This newly emergent Left movement was in favor of equal rights and justice for all people, the abolition of slavery, the end of epidemic religious beliefs (Voltaire's battle cry of the Enlightenment was "Remember the cruelties!"—the intense cruelties inflicted by the church on millions of people, all in the name of a loving God—and the Left generally supported the end of premodern mythic religion and its replacement by modern rational science), major support for individual rights and free speech, and a government that followed suit, with the end of monarchy itself and the beginning of democratic forms of governance. On the other side of the aisle, the old, traditional, "Right" political party that the Left was against believed, indeed, in the already existing traditional, conventional society and what had worked for it, including its form of governance and its strongly held traditional religious beliefs, as well as a social structure including monarchy, aristocratic upper classes, serfs, and slaves, all set on a patriarchal and deeply mythic-religious foundation.

For the next several hundred years, these two major political belief systems vied for control (Whigs and Tories, Democrats and Republicans, etc.). Then, starting in the sixties, as we have seen, a fundamentally new and different stage of development began to emerge, and this new stage created a significantly different type of political belief. It was the emergence of green, and this political view was aggressively devoted to ending all remaining oppression of any marginalized group; it was hugely invested in protecting the environment against any and all threats (as such, it often stood in conflict with the business-and-profit orientation of the previous orange modern/capitalist stage and insisted on "sustainability economics"); it backed all forms of feminism (orange had supported and originally created feminism, but green took to it zealously, along with all other anti-oppression movements, from the Black Panthers to Black Lives Matter to LGBTQ rights); and it was in favor of curtailing the free speech of individuals if it harmed any minority group. Both orange and green were worldcentric, but apart from that, their interests differed in many profound and significant ways.

The addition of a new and fundamental stage of human development threw each of the two major political parties into a significant degree of internal turmoil. The progressive Left, precisely because it was progressive, or tended to follow new evolutionary unfoldings, was now divided between its original, foundational values of the Enlightenment—individual rights and freedom; universal values of life, liberty, and the pursuit of happiness; the separation of church and state; emphasis on individual free speech and individual freedom in general—versus the novel values of newly emerging green: overall, an emphasis on green's "equality" above and over orange's "freedom," and thus an emphasis on group rights and a curtailing of individual rights if they in any way threaten to marginalize or even offend any minority group (including a direct challenge to the First Amendment and a willingness to limit free speech if it seemed to hurt the feelings of any group); an emphasis on "earth equality!" and environmental protections (even if it might hurt the freedom of humans); actively promoting marginalized groups over similarly qualified others (sometimes including actual quotas, and at least affirmative action). These two sets of values were vaguely in the same worldcentric ballpark, but when it came to specifics, they were often night and day. From that point onward, the Left (and the Democratic Party) was involved in an internal fight over which of these two major value sets (modern orange versus postmodern green) would actually determine policy. It is still a battle that is perfectly obvious to anybody who looks through this lens.

And the same thing, a notch down, was happening with the Right (and the Republicans). Their foundational base had always been amber, and thus they had more ethnocentric beliefs than progressives—rightly or wrongly, they were seen to be more racist, more sexist, more hyper-patriotic and nationalistic, more patriarchal, more militaristic, more xenophobic, more homophobic, and much more religiously fundamentalist or "mythic-literal"— and they themselves often openly championed such values. But with the shift upward of evolution itself, which had added a new level, the leading-edge of the Right also notched up a stage. As the Left had added a green branch to its orange foundation, the Right added an orange branch to its amber foundation. This new group on the Right was often called "Wall Street Republicans" (reflecting its embrace of orange progress, achievement, and profit), and hence it aggressively embraced many values that once were embraced solely by the Enlightenment or "old" liberals (for their "newness" they were sometimes called "neoconservatives" or just "neocons"). This political movement was zealously in favor of big business and anything that would help it and its orange profits; it fought for worldcentric individual rights against ethnocentric-favoring group "liberal" moves and associated "identity politics" (which indeed had too often caught the ongoing green regression from worldcentric to ethnocentric-favoring); it disliked government enormously (because it was too often run by liberals pushing green egalitarian rights and massive social entitlements); and it supported free speech against political correctness with a passion edging into libertarianism. The Republican Party, like the Democratic, split into two major camps, reflecting the overall path of evolution itself—in this case, the "base" or "old" Right (strongly amber ethnocentric) and the "new" Right (orange business-profit-individual rights worldcentric).

When it came to employment, it turned out that, whether it was an orange or green Democrat, they weren't as in favor of business as the Republican (orange or amber). (More granularly, reflecting their actual levels, the orange wing of both the Democrat and Republican parties usually supported Wall Street, while the green wing of liberals opposed it, often with more socialistic, anti-capitalist, anti-orange agendas.) Traditionally, when it came to an actual division between business management and business laborers, the Democrats (favoring the worldcentric "masses") supported employees and unions against management, but with the ongoing failure of the leading-edge, the typical worker eventually did not feel supported by the Democrats at all. In fact, in the 2016 election, especially the lower-level employees went substantially for Trump. He actually pitched to that group, and did so in a very ethnocentric fashion: he would protect jobs at home, punish companies that went abroad, heavily tax products coming in from overseas companies, and "make America great again"—hyper-patriotic, ethnocentric, amber to the core. As has often been noted, some 70 percent of whites with only a high school education or lower voted for Trump.

Cementing his appeal to ethnocentric, some 60 percent of white voters in general went for Trump, including an astonishing 53 percent of white women (a higher percentage of white women than any Republican nominee in recent memory—and not just those with a "lower education": 45 percent of all college-educated white women voted Trump). On the mythic-literal side of ethnocentric—or the "evangelicals"—over 80 percent of those voters chose Trump (and this especially shows how beliefs trumped realities, because there is precious little religious about "Mr. Two Corinthians" Trump). The whole point here is how these background stages of worldview development have a hidden but enormously powerful hand in all this. Another 81 percent of the voters who defined themselves as "angry" went Trump, and not just the lower education or lower income vote. In fact, the median income of a Trump voter was $71,000.

In short, of the 60 percent of the population that is ethnocentric (or lower), the vast majority of them seem to have gone for Trump, and in a stunning fashion. Many of them indicated that he was "unqualified" (60 percent), that he mistreated women (55 percent), even that he was unstable (45 percent), and yet a majority of all of those voted for him anyway.

Clearly, something else was going on. An amazing 70 percent of those who described themselves as wanting "change" voted Trump. The vast majority of change-agents voting Trump? Normally that would sound progressive, wouldn't it? A full 81 percent of those who described themselves as "angry" went Trump. Astonishing. We saw another 80 percent of evangelicals went Trump. Even nearly half of those who claimed that the "country is on the wrong track" voted Trump. Where are those huge numbers coming from? Almost any factors we use to explain one of those don't really explain the others.

But what does explain them all is that, in addition to the specifics driving each of those voting blocs themselves, there was another factor, an additional factor, that was at play in all of them: a powerful anti-green field that reverberated through each and every one of those areas; and Trump's loud, aggressive, daily anti-green sentiments added an additional push that greatly activated, increased, and drove each of those areas toward high percentage points favoring Trump, and often in amounts verging on outrageous. The anti-green morphic field was a very broad coattail upon which Trump (not as a conscious and rational decision, but as a very broad background intuition) rode to a victory that stunned almost everybody, including his own people. Whether Trump was directly activating and appealing to red, or to amber, or to orange, he was always also riding anti-green.

It's time to look at this anti-green field a little more closely. If it is indeed the central overarching key to Trump's victory, understanding it will be crucial to helping to determine any genuinely effective responses. And failing to do so—and remaining merely in a "protester" or "resister" role—will simply keep us operating in exactly the rut that evolution's self-correction is seeking to surpass—we ourselves, in short, become part of what evolution is attempting to overcome.

5 : The Reverberating Anti-Green Field

What virtually all of Trump's voters had in common was resentment—they resented the cultural elite, whether in government or universities or "on the coasts," and they wanted . . . if "revenge" is the wrong word, it's not far off. But there was, I am suggesting, another and very strong, hidden current in all of this, and that was the anti-green morphic field—the antagonistic reaction and turning-away tendency generated by a leading-edge that had gone deeply sour and dysfunctional, and wasn't even serving the 25 percent of the population that were themselves at green. The deeply self-contradictory nature of "there-is-no-truth" green had collapsed the very leading-edge of evolution itself, had jammed it, had derailed it, and in a bruised, confused but inherently wisdom-driven series of moves, evolution was backing up, regrouping, and looking for ways to move forward. This included activating an amber ethnocentric wave that, in addition to being inherently anti-green, had always been present and very powerful but had, for the most part, been denied direct control of society starting around a century or so ago (as orange and then green stepped in as leading-edges). When a Republican had been placed in power, which was relatively often, it was usually an orange-leaning Republican (with mandatory amber ethnocentric sub-beliefs, but talking worldcentric language).

But Trump, like no politician in anybody's memory, directly hit the amber nerve. (And every anti-green sentiment out of

Trump's mouth helped add to his score with amber.) He literally and deliberately spoke in amber ethnocentric terms—thinly veiled (if veiled at all) racist, sexist, openly patriarchal, ubernationalistic, misogynistic, jingoistic, and on and on in ways that literally had critics' mouths dropped wide open. People simply could not believe the stuff coming out of Trump—especially since they could not see the complete traffic jam lying up ahead at the leading-edge, where direction had collapsed completely in a rampant case of aperspectival madness that was reverberating all the way down the entire spectrum of development. Again, it wasn't just that Trump was ethnocentric (although it was that royally), it was that his every move was also deeply anti-green, and Trump's own anti-green current caught the powerful anti-green wave radiating from the leading-edge itself.

Trump's anti-green impulse runs serious, far, and vast (though he consciously is aware of none of this). Whether his proposals are red or amber or orange, they are always also anti-green. And that is the one thing they all have in common, whether they are red, amber, or orange—they are all energized in part by this anti-green self-correcting drive of evolution in search of a functional and self-organizing way forward (and a way that allows each of these stages an actual participation in the overall national dialogue, and doesn't aggressively deny and ridicule any of them as being merely "deplorable"). As we'll explore in a moment, amber was activated because it needed to find a way to be integrated into a larger society in a way that had been denied it for a very long time. Any specifically amber moves themselves are not directly part of the overall self-correcting drive of evolution, but the activation of amber itself most definitely is—and its voice desperately needs to be heard. It needs to be "transcended," most certainly, but it also—and this is the lesson here—needs to be "included," if evolution is to return to its general functional and self-organizing drive of "transcend and include." That is the secret, hidden, but very real drive that Trump unconsciously rode to a victory that, because its primary driver was completely unseen, was a total shock to both camps and to every major pollster in existence.

Trump is so boisterously amber ethnocentric in so many ways, this will force the present green leading-edge into one of two major reactions: it will simply double down on its present hatred, revulsion, and open ridicule of amber (aimed at Trump and followers), or it will pause, realize that its own hatred and ridicule of amber has profoundly contributed to amber's angry, virulent, hateful resentment of elites everywhere, and hence realize that it must in some ways attempt to understand, include, even compassionately embrace that large portion of the population whom green is in fact supposed to be leading, not despising. If it takes the former route, then the overarching anti-green atmosphere will simply energize amber to force its way into the mainstream, ethnocentric power drives and all, and an increasing series of disasters will inevitably follow. If it takes the latter route, it will be aligning itself with the self-corrective drive of evolution itself as it looks for a more inclusive and comprehensive base platform from which to again take up its leading-edge role of self-organization through self-transcendence, or transcending and *truly* including. (More about this later.)

In the meantime, Trump is being driven not only by his red egocentric narcissism, not only by his amber ethnocentrism (especially noticeable), and not only by his occasional orange worldcentrism, but always also by this overarching morphogenetic anti-green field. Trump intends to virtually eliminate a good number of environmental regulations (i.e., anti-green); his selection of Scott Pruitt as head of the Environmental Protection Agency already has every environmental organization in the world completely alarmed (i.e., anti-green). He intends to increase military spending enormously, including re-engaging the nuclear arms race (anti-green). He will severely limit immigration, with particular emphasis on Mexicans and Muslims (anti-green). He will lower taxes, including on the very wealthy (anti-green). He will roll back an estimated 60 to 70 percent of business regulations (anti-green). He will devastate foreign trade agreements, and cut into any international unification project around (anti-green). He will repeal Obamacare (anti-green).

Those are pretty much most of Trump's major stated policy plans, and whatever else they are, and they are many things, they are all—every single one of them—a massive kick in the face of green.

Thus, although Trump's main constituency is that 60 percent of America (rich or poor, educated or not) whose basic center of gravity is ethnocentric amber, even when he activates standard orange business/achievement/profit currents, it's usually through the dismantling of some rule or regulation that the green leading-edge has previously put in place. Trump is intentionally anti-political-correctness. His "make America great again" is to be accomplished by basically undoing most of the items that a leading-edge green government has put into place, as it looked to "help" or "protect" individuals but also primarily to "deconstruct" divisive boundaries wherever they existed. Thus, leading-edge green had moved to undo restrictive trade agreements so that it would become easier to draw in large portions of the world by making it easier to commercially cross American boundaries—and Trump plans to end those. And he wants to undo immigration regulations that were trying to lower the boundaries to any immigrants (Hillary Clinton's ideas on dramatically opening immigration were particularly galling to Trump). He wants to make it harder on terrorists by strengthening the borders that we do have. He wants to undo green's relaxation of military spending and lowering of military boundaries everywhere. Trump, in every direction, wants to re-entrench the boundaries that a leading-edge green had actively deconstructed. (Obama was criticized, even by his supporters, for tending to lack a certain "firmness," especially in his foreign policy, such as his allowing NASA to promote pro-Muslim efforts and his possibly too-lenient stance with Iran. In short, a bit of his own deep green tendencies showed their aperspectival madness in a lack of directiveness or "firmness." All of these green moves were aggressively condemned by Trump.)

Now, I'm not saying that what Trump is doing is right. What he is doing is basically ethnocentric, and has to be judged itself in exactly that light. But I am saying that the *reason* he is doing much of what he is doing is concomitantly driven by a background anti-green morphogenetic field, which has been created as the green leading-edge drowned in a swamp of aperspectival madness, and hence failed significantly to be a genuine leading-edge—it failed to provide any leading direction at all (but rather just a deconstruction of things already in place), because in losing all "truth," it lost all compass points. All this eventually led to a necessary self-correcting drive of stepping back, refurbishing, and reorganizing in an attempt to create a truly self-organizing dynamic that will allow it to move forward once again. It's as if you bit into an apple and hit a rusty nail and chipped your leading-edge incisor— the one thing you don't do is keep biting.

In short, whether Trump was activating red egocentric, or amber ethnocentric, or orange worldcentric, he was always also anti-green. And the anti-green current (acting in a preconscious fashion in the dynamics of ongoing cultural evolution) would allow all of these stages to find their station energized by something Trump was doing. It's an astonishing amalgamation— indeed, one that many analysts claim is unique in all of American politics. Never had an "anti" stance reached out and energized so many stages—because never before had the leading-edge so blatantly failed to lead. And the overall meta-drive in all of this is to find a way that all of these previous stages can actually be heard, and truly seen, and more effectively and compassionately integrated into the larger currents of cultural evolution in a way that green (with its aggressively deconstructive aperspectival madness) has profoundly failed to do.

Whether Trump was activating red, amber, or orange (with amber ethnocentric being central), there were many other currents that combined with his general anti-green dynamic to determine how each wave that was being activated by Trump was indeed activated (that is, factors not only from the different levels but also different quadrants, different lines, and different states are all involved in this).

As for orange, business factors almost always interacted with those currents that concerned orange economic factors in general, and the widespread sense that Trump was a businessman tended to make some orange business people feel attracted to him (and it certainly attracted unemployed workers who felt Trump would "bring back jobs"); after his election, Wall Street did indeed shoot north. Others, of course, tended to point out that Trump had failed in business many more times than he had succeeded. Either way, Trump is the first president in American history who was elected with essentially no experience in either politics or the military and also is not a lawyer, but comes almost solely from a business background. (So that the way he conducted business is likely the way he will conduct government, which doesn't make too many people feel comfortable.)

In other words, orange-level realities do loom prominently in the Trumpian constellation. This definitely includes the military-industrial complex, as displayed in Trump's major appointments to the highest positions, which were very heavily drawn particularly from three sources: Wall Street, fossil-fuel business, and the military—the swamp he promised to drain doesn't seem to be going away anytime soon. (This orange factor includes those critics who see turmoil in the "Deep State" and "Deep System" as primarily driving Trump's election, and, indeed, those who see techno-economic realities in general as being crucial. I'm making

abundant room for those in the list of essentially orange-level—
and Lower-Right quadrant—facts and realities; I'm also claiming
that they are not centrally as major as the background anti-green
field.)

Looking now at amber, it is the ethnocentric crowd that, in
addition to being the primary level of attraction, have perhaps the
most number of other variables working in favor of their activation:
their race, their sex, technological currents, governmental drivers,
economic factors, cultural resentment. Trump's success has most
often been attributed to a great white male underclass. While that
is only one factor, and a big one, it is nevertheless only part of the
overall picture. But it's true that this class has been stereotyped in
especially nasty ways by the elite—primarily by the green leading-
edge. They are everything that Hillary Clinton meant when she
tellingly (and with sincere conviction) called Trump's supporters "a basket of deplorables." This group is viewed as the single,
great, rednecked, oafish, uneducated, gigantic instigator of oppression of all minorities. This large white lower class somehow
has oppressed and disenfranchised African Americans, women,
gays and lesbians, the disabled, Latinos, Asians, and "real" for-
eigners (like Mexicans and Muslims, not like the white Irish or
Germans, who have become part of the oppressors), and they are
said to loathe and hate anybody not of their race, sex, blood, origins, or creed.

We'll address whether that is true or not in a moment, but
it is true that this "underclass," as it is most often characterized
(white, male, lower education, lower class, rural), did indeed vote
for Trump in a big way. The massive resentment that they had
developed, the anger at being looked at by the leading elites as
"deplorables" (which the elite most certainly did), was a festering
sore spot that Trump's every anti-green salvo tended to soothe
mightily, a wondrous balm for lacerated souls. Far from getting
upset by any of these tirades (which virtually every green always
did, and vocally), they loved Trump for this. Even with many of

them feeling he was "unqualified," "misogynistic," or even "unstable," they voted for him en masse. Nothing, no matter how embarrassing (which Trump committed in outlandish ways almost daily, each seemingly worse than its predecessor, right up to the staggeringly adolescent—and criminal—"grab them by the pussy" videotape)—none of it fundamentally mattered, because Trump was spouting a heartfelt, anti-green, "truthful" sentiment, and this crowd truly loved him for it. Decades of being treated as white trash—with all of its ressentiment—was being washed away with every idiocy, and they simply could not get enough.

And as for energizing the red egocentric crowd—well, that more or less speaks for itself. Paraphrasing Arthur Lovejoy, there is no human stupidity that has not found its champion, and narcissists everywhere found in Trump a resounding champion.

6 : The Primary Cause—
and Cure—of Oppression

et's briefly touch on this issue of oppression, the complete ending of which is perhaps green's strongest central goal. Although the ideal itself is totally commendable (and happens to be
one I fully support), the problem comes when a flatland aperspectival madness attempts to understand the source, cause, and cure
of oppression itself. And you can just guess, right from the start,
that this is not going to have a happy ending.

Green will typically look at history, for example, and whenever it finds a society in which there is a widespread *lack* of green
values, it assumes that these green values would normally and
naturally be present were it not for the fact that they have been
maliciously oppressed by the dominator hierarchies found in that
society. All individuals would possess worldcentric green values
of pluralism, radical egalitarianism, and total equality, except for
the oppressive controlling powers that crush those values wherever they appear. Looking at history carefully, green found a lack
of these values going all the way back to day one, and thus the
assumption was made that a massively oppressive force (or group
of them) was present from the start of humankind's life on this
planet, and these oppressive forces are still operating everywhere
today, and thus green's job of ending discrimination, marginalization, misogyny, homophobia, and endless varieties of enslavement is an ongoing, difficult, yet desperately urgent chore, which
is mightily resisted by the powers that be at every turn.

The existence of strong and widespread oppressive forces cannot be doubted. The problem comes in the claim to know what their source and cause is. For green postmodernism, the lack of worldcentric green values in any culture is due to an aggressive and intensively active repressive and oppressive force, usually the male sex itself (via ever-present patriarchy) or a particular race (white in most parts of the world, coupled with a rampant colonialism) and/or due to a particular creed (usually religious fundamentalism of one sort or another, mostly Christian), oppressive economic factors (almost always capitalism), and finally, various prejudices: against gays, against women, against whatever minority that is oppressed. All told, it is basic postmodern dogma that humanity has always been subjected to oppression and unfreedom, and this is due to any of a list of various "isms" that the evil side of humanity falls prey to regularly if not aggressively monitors and sanctions: androcentrism, phallocentrism, logocentrism, phallologocentrism, racism, eurocentrism, misogynism, patriarchy, speciesism, sexism, supremacism, nationalism, patriotism, orientalism, technologism, capitalism—what they all have in common is that they are some of the many ways that green values can be, and have been, mightily denied and oppressed throughout history, and continue to be in today's world.

In short, green staunchly believes that a *lack* of green values (egalitarian, group freedom, gender equality, human care and sensitivity) is due to a *presence* of oppression. Lack of green = presence of oppression. This lack goes all the way back to day one, and thus various strong oppressive currents have been present from day one, and continue now in alarmingly widespread ways. Note that it is not the presence of oppression that is being denied here—various forms of oppression have indeed been present almost from the start. What is being questioned here is green's firm belief that its own green values would be widely flourishing if given an even chance, and the major reason that they are not is due to the fact that they have been, and are being, oppressed—and this oppression goes all the way back through human history. So the corollary issue here is, if green values are not present, and the cause of that lack is definitely not oppression, then what is the real cause, why aren't they available? (The one variation on this theme is the openly romantic version: that some very early stages of human development were largely free of oppression—that cultures such as magic foraging tribal ones were egalitarian and "partnership" societies, but then at some point a new evolutionary development—either amber agriculture or orange industrialization—introduced severe oppressive forces. But in either version, the same basic belief remains central: lack of green = presence of oppression.)

The major problem with that view, taken by itself, is that it completely overlooks the actual data on the role of growth, development, and evolution. We've already seen that human moral identity grows and develops from egocentric (red) to ethnocentric (amber) to worldcentric (orange then green) to integral (turquoise), and this is true individually as well as collectively/historically. Thus, the *main* reason that slavery was present, say, 2,000 years ago, is not because there was an oppressive force preventing worldcentric freedom, but that a worldcentric notion of freedom had not even emerged yet anywhere on the planet. (It never dawned on somebody that a group or race that was fully "other" should even be treated as "equal"—for the most part, that thought just never arose; it was never an issue to be seriously wrestled with; that type of "equality" was a value that crossed virtually nobody's mind.) It wasn't present and then oppressed, as green imagines; it simply had not yet emerged in the first place—there were no green-stage values anywhere to oppress. This is why, as only one example, all of the world's Great Religions, which otherwise teach love and compassion and treating all beings kindly, nonetheless— precisely because they were created during the great *ethnocentric* Mythic Age of traditional civilization—had no extensive and widespread conception of the fundamental worldcentric freedom of human beings, or a belief that all humans, regardless of race, sex, color, or creed, were born equal (a belief that emerged with widespread orange and was even more fervently celebrated by green). In Greek society in Athens, vaunted home of democracy, 1 out of 3 people were slaves—and there was no effective complaint on a culture-wide scale. Nor was there ever a widespread culturally effective complaint lodged by Christianity or Buddhism or Hinduism or the others. (Saint Paul recommends to slaves that they accept Jesus and happily obey their master.) It wasn't until the emergence of the orange worldcentric Age of Reason (a mere 300 years ago) that "we hold these truths to be self-evident, that all men are created equal" actually came into existence—emerged evolutionarily—and thus started to be believed by the average and typical member of that culture. A war like the War between the States—fought in part because of that realization—was unthinkable anywhere a thousand years earlier; it just would have made no sense.

Slavery was first invented and practiced by black men on black men in Africa, simply because this is where humans first emerged, then spread basically everywhere and through all races, starting with the earliest tribes themselves, which, whenever they actually ran into each other, usually sparked warfare or slavery— as we saw, 15 percent of indigenous tribes practiced slavery, and they did so because worldcentric morality had not yet emerged on a wide scale—hence this unfreedom is not primarily due to the presence of an oppressive force but to the *absence of a higher development*. Oppression is not in any way its primary cause, and if it is treated as if it were, then the "cures" that are enforced will never—*never*—actually work, because the real cause has gone undetected and thus continues to exist and operate under the surface. And the real cause is not the presence of oppression but the lack of development.

So in this particular regard, it is not true that lack of green = presence of oppression; it is that lack of green = lack of development. As noted, oppression indeed existed; but that is not at all why green itself did not exist. Green didn't exist, not because of a countervailing *force*, but because it had not yet *emerged* at all—in this regard, there was nothing to oppress. People are not born with green values; those values are rather the product of 5 or 6 major stages of human growth and development, and prior to their actual emergence, they don't exist anywhere they could actually be oppressed in the first place.

This is true across the board—oppression related to race, sex, creed, gender. Think of feminist Carol Gilligan's stages of female moral development. Gilligan became an overnight feminist icon with her remarkable book *In a Different Voice*, which was pioneering for two major assertions that it made. The first is that when it comes to moral reasoning, men and women tend to think differently. Men tend to emphasize autonomy, rights, and justice, and women tend to emphasize relationship, care, and responsibility—in short, men tend to emphasize agency and hierarchy (ranking), whereas women tend to emphasize communion and relationship (nonranking). Since feminists usually equated any and all hierarchies with social oppression, it seemed clear that men (and the patriarchy) were responsible for virtually all of society's ills. This point in the book was eagerly and widely adopted by most feminists. But the second major point in the book was studiously avoided by most feminists: namely, that both men and women tend to develop through four major hierarchical stages of thinking (her terms). In other words, women's nonhierarchical thinking itself grows and develops through four hierarchical stages. Virtually no feminist repeated that point.

What Gilligan had stumbled upon was a truth now widely acknowledged by virtually all developmentalists: namely, that there are two major but very different types of hierarchies, usually called *dominator hierarchies* and *growth hierarchies*. Dominator hierarchies are all the nasty things that postmodern multiculturalists say they are: oppressive, power-driven, suffering-inducing, dominating. We see these in everything from the caste system to *la cosa nostra*–style criminal rings to slave networks everywhere. In these dominator hierarchies, the higher you go, the more people you can control and oppress. Growth hierarchies, on the other hand, *are exactly the opposite.* Where each higher level in a dominator hierarchy is more excluding and more oppressive, each higher level in a growth hierarchy is more inclusive and less oppressive (or, stated conversely, is more loving—and we actually have empirical research demonstrating this). Because of their unifying and integrating nature, growth hierarchies are often called "holarchies." The evolutionary leaps that we are looking at in this presentation—the major developmental stages from egocentric to ethnocentric to worldcentric to integral—is exactly a type of growth holarchy. Each higher level is more inclusive, more caring, more loving, more conscious, and more embracing.

The archetypal growth holarchy in nature is the one that unites all of its fundamental units: this holarchy goes from quarks to atoms to molecules to cells to organisms. Each of those levels "transcends and includes"—it both transcends (or goes beyond) and includes (or fully enwraps) its predecessor: a whole quark is part of an atom; a whole atom is part of a molecule; a whole molecule is part of a cell; a whole cell is part of an organism. Each level is a whole that is a part of the next-higher whole. Arthur Koestler calls each of these units a "holon," or a "whole/part," a whole that is also a part of a larger whole. Reality in general is composed primarily of holons.

The central point is that, with these growth holarchies, the higher level does not oppress or enslave or dominate the lower level; it enfolds it, it includes it, it embraces it—if anything, it loves it. Cells don't despise molecules, molecules don't hate atoms—again, if anything, they love them, they embrace them. And the whole of evolution (at least as it has appeared so far) is the construction of these ever-higher, ever more whole, more unified, and more integrated elements—wholes that are parts of ever-higher wholes. This is the "order out of chaos"—the Eros—that leading-edge science sees as an inherent drive in the universe at large. And more to the point for us, it is an inherent drive in human beings as well—and any sane and comprehensive overview of human growth and development (not to mention any attempts at effective "social engineering") would want to take these growth holarchies into account, starting right at the beginning.

(This doesn't mean that every higher level is nothing but "sweetness and light." Something can, and usually does, go wrong at every level, and the more levels you have, the more things that can go wrong. We'll return to that; but for now, we're focusing on the fact that each higher level, by definition, brings the *potential* for greater diversity, more care, and more inclusiveness, and that's a trend we want to follow. Because if that is the major way that more diversity and real inclusiveness is actually produced, then the rabid denial of growth hierarchies—by the green postmodern leading-edge—actually has the disastrous effect of severely limiting the production of any genuine diversity and true inclusiveness at all. That truly disturbing fact is perhaps the very core of broken green's actual brokenness. This might be quite important, yes?)

Thus, it is no surprise that Carol Gilligan, while directly researching men and women's growth and development, found a growth hierarchy of four major levels of moral development—each more inclusive. Now, I've already given a quick meta-summary of the overall stages of human growth and development (simplified as archaic to magic to mythic to rational to pluralistic to integral), and I pointed out that, in looking at over a hundred models of human development, you can fairly constantly see these same basic 6-to-8 major levels of development being recognized time and time again by various researchers. Some models have a few more stages, some have a few less, but you can see the same basic 6-to-8 appear again and again. In this presentation, we're using a simplified half dozen major stages: crimson archaic (the earliest transition stage from the great apes), magenta magic (or impulsive), red magic-mythic (or power), amber mythic (or ethnocentric traditional values), orange rational (or modern values), green pluralistic (or postmodern values), and turquoise integral (or the first truly synthesizing and integrating level). I have further simplified and summarized these as *egocentric* (archaic and magic), *ethnocentric* (mythic), *worldcentric* (orange modern and green postmodern), and *kosmocentric* (or truly integral).

Gilligan directly discovered these same four basic generalized stages. What is nice about her model is its simplicity; the fact that she clearly understands the difference between dominator hierarchies and growth hierarchies; and that, as a postmodern feminist in good standing, she is an excellent example of how growth holarchies are mandatory in getting a truly profound and comprehensive view of virtually any human issue or problem. And her major point is that, although both men and women go through the same basic four stages of holarchical growth, they each do so "in a different voice," and hence psychologists need to stop using the male voice as if it covered all human options. Gilligan would be the first to acknowledge that all human beings have a full spectrum of both voices; these are only generalized averages. In these days of greatly increased gender awareness— including gay, lesbian, bisexual, transgendered, and "non-binary" sexual orientations—"essentialism" (or the belief in rigid and fixed categories of anything) is as outdated as DOS.

With all of that in mind, here are the stages that Gilligan discovered, in simple generalizations. Stage 1 she called *selfish*, where the woman cares only for herself (our red **egocentric**). Stage 2 she called the *care* stage, where the woman extends care to her chosen group, and then has a strong "us versus them" attitude (a genuine care, but care for just "my group—my race, sex, class, tribe, nation, creed—versus all those *others* who are different from me," our amber **ethnocentric**). Then stage 3 is the *universal care* stage (not just "care" but "*universal* care"), where the woman cares for all groups, for all humans (our orange and green **worldcentric**). And stage 4 she called *integrated*, where the woman integrates both masculine and feminine modes in herself (our turquoise **integral**). Only starting at the worldcentric stage of *universal care* would the woman begin to find something like oppression or marginalization truly objectionable; otherwise, it's just the hand you're dealt. There is no universal objection to oppression until the universal stage itself, and thus this objection is not something that is present from the beginning and subsequently squashed, but something that must emerge as growth and development continues. (And this is why, although humans have been on this planet for some 500,000 years, we only outlawed slavery a mere 200 years ago—it required the emergence of a *universal* care stage, which is why it took so unimaginably long.)

So let's look at how including a developmental perspective profoundly alters virtually any problem we are looking at. Gilligan is a feminist, so let's look at a feminist issue—and this will show, I trust, how important this idea is, even in a discipline such as feminism, which usually denies—and often deeply dislikes—all hierarchies whatsoever. For example, it's common to hear nowadays that, because of an overly patriarchal trend in Western culture, what Western culture needs desperately is a massive influx of feminine values. We hear this a lot, yes? But notice that what Western culture most definitely does *not* need are more of the feminine values at stage 1 and stage 2. More narcissistic and more racist/sexist values are exactly what Western culture needs less of—and yet those are precisely the feminine values at stage 1 and stage 2 (which also happen to be the most common stages). What people mean when they say, "We need more feminine values," is that we need more stage-3 and stage-4 feminine values, more worldcentric and integral feminine values, not more narcissistic and racist/sexist values (a belief I fully share). But see how this issue is dramatically changed when we include a developmental perspective?

So, to pick up our story: If we think that green values (of

stage-3 universal care) should naturally and normally be found everywhere, and their lack unerringly indicates an oppressive force, then we will see nothing but victims everywhere (simply because green is one of the very highest stages of development yet to emerge, and all the previous stages by definition lack green, and if that lack always misguidedly means oppression, then all of those stages are mistakenly viewed as oppressed "victims"—and thus the numbers of oppressed victims absolutely explodes). And our cure for this will not be to instigate factors that will help with growth and development, but to punish and criminalize those at the lower stages of development who are acting in oppressive ways. As we just saw with dominator hierarchies and growth holarchies, only at egocentric selfish and ethnocentric care stages will someone want to oppress and hold others down to begin with, but when worldcentric green sees such actions, it assumes that an oppressor somewhere is attempting to oppress free and equal worldcentric conditions— and this gets the entire dynamic backward.

Put differently, oppressive actions and drives are inherent in the lower stages of development. As we saw, dominator hierarchies are inherent at the lower stages of growth hierarchies—that is, at egocentric and ethnocentric, which are inherently domineering—and they vanish at the higher stages of growth hierarchies—worldcentric and integral, which are *universally* caring. It's not that higher stages are incapable of malevolent or oppressive actions; they are not. But they are not *inherently* oppressive, oppressive as part of their intrinsic structure—when such behavior occurs in higher stages, it is due to idiosyncratic *shadow* issues, and has to be dealt with on a case-by-case basis; its frequency, in any event, is vastly less than at egocentric/ethnocentric. In short, the primary cure for dominator hierarchies is to move to the higher stages of growth hierarchies. A lower, pre-worldcentric stage of development will step all over worldcentric values if it can, not because it is trying to specifically oppress those values, but because it does not yet possess those values itself and has no understanding of their value, goodness, or desirability. The cure for this is to move development forward, not to criminalize earlier stages (which is like calling age 5 a disease and outlawing it).

It is certainly the case that a society can choose to pass laws against any behavior that has the effect of oppressing other beings—and there is every reason to do so. But when it comes to the *cause* of that opppressing behavior, in addition to factors that come from every quadrant (including Lower-Right economic factors, Lower-Right technological factors, and Upper-Right brain physiology—which flatland exterior approaches usually acknowledge), it is mandatory that *interior dimensions* also be fully taken into account (including Lower-Left ethical development and Upper-Left moral development—or the various levels and stages of actual growth). To simply see intentional "oppressors" and their "victims" everywhere is to catastrophically mis-diagnose (and thus mis-treat) the illness.

Hence, as for that "basket of deplorables," to the extent that they are genuinely at amber, ethnocentric, premodern stages of development, they are uncomfortable with worldcentric values (orange and green), not because they fully see them and loathe them, but because they do not (and cannot) see them in the first place. As Kegan puts it, such values are "over their heads." This truly is not meant in a judgmental fashion but simply as an explanatory and descriptive narrative, because the cure here involves not hating them and "deploring" them and criminalizing them (unless their behavior in itself warrants such), but to reach out and compassionately include them in the ongoing national dialogue and ongoing cultural normative development—which is precisely what the green leading-edge (including its Hillary champions) have actively refused to do for at least four or five decades now.

Is it really any wonder that half of this country now hates the other half?

And here lies green's performative contradiction. Green

officially will perceive nobody as being fundamentally "lower" or "needing to actually grow," because to suggest that any group truly needs to increase its developmental depth—implying that some levels are "better" or "higher" than others—is to be guilty, in a world of aperspectival madness and extreme political correctness, of being "racist" or "sexist" or some other horrible crime against humanity. No stance is recognized as superior to any other, and there certainly is no such thing as a "higher" or "better" level or stance—that's just the utterly taboo and horrid *ranking*. (We want "partnership" societies, not "ranking" societies—which apparently means that ethnocentric and worldcentric values are to be held in equal partnership, that "equality" and "racist/sexist" values are to be given equal weight in real partnership.) Yet although green itself is the product of five or six major developmental stages, *it allows this development for nobody*—even to suggest such "ranking" or "judging" is totally anathema—which is nothing but a colossal and massive failure, due to aperspectival madness, of the leading-edge.

And yet, as we are starting to see, although green will not allow the existence of any "higher" or "better" levels or views, it still deeply feels that its own views are definitely "higher" and "better"—and, to the extent that its views are in fact representing, for example, worldcentric over ethnocentric views, they are indeed fundamentally higher and better (precisely because they are more inclusive and less domineering and oppressive)! But this is exactly what green cannot officially admit or acknowledge—hence its being caught in a performative contradiction and collapsing as a conscious and functional leading-edge.

And more to the point, when this developmental increase in capacity for inclusiveness, care, and compassion is officially not acknowledged, then it seeps out in disguised and often disgusted ways (because you keep intuiting the existence of these factually "higher" realities, even if your worldview tries to deny any such ranking, so they force their way into awareness, twisted as they might be). Green gets so infuriated at its own self-contradictory stance (for example, even to think that your egalitarian view is a better way to view things is to contradict egalitarianism right at the start!), and so you end up blurting out your conclusion in malevolent, even vicious ways. To give the most notorious example, Hillary said, in effect, "[By comparison to *me*,] they're all a basket of deplorables!" This was a horridly botched and utterly inept attempt to say, "These worldcentric, all-embracing values that I am trying to represent are better, more inclusive and more caring, than those ethnocentric and excluding views that Trump has been proudly proclaiming." But given that even this statement itself would directly and unmistakably contradict the central dogma of green—that is, aperspectival madness, no judging or ranking— Hillary had no idea how to actually, genuinely, and inoffensively state beliefs that every liberal embraces. And that is just the start of broken green's problems.

We'll come back to this central issue—and its cure—in part three. For now, simply note that green multiculturalism has an intense and absolutely believed *judgment* that worldcentric all-inclusive views are categorically better than ethnocentric power-driven and oppressive views—but it also has an overriding belief that judgments themselves are inherently oppressive and evil ("nothing is superior, no nasty ranking or judging!"), and thus, slamming into its own performative contradiction, it cannot give any legitimate and coherent reasons that its views carry any substantial weight (if nothing really is superior, neither is its own view claiming that, and thus there's no compelling reason to adopt it at all). And it has a *hierarchical ranking* that worldcentric all-inclusive views are categorically better and higher than ethnocentric oppressive views—but again, it has an overriding belief that all hierarchies are domineering and coercive, and thus, once again smashing into its own performative contradiction (namely, aperspectival madness), it cannot coherently argue for its own beliefs, so it merely stammers out, yells out, that its opponents are all "Fascists! Racists! Sexists! Privileged! Oppressors!" Their arguments, at their core, have many valid (i.e., superior) points, but because of their overriding belief in aperspectival madness (and "no truth"), they shoot themselves in the foot (or more often, the head), right at the start of their discussion—and thus have become a largely broken, collapsed, fragmented leading-edge.

So when it comes to oppressive and domineering forces, the problem that green slams into is that it officially looks at all individuals in an egalitarian fashion—which means it simply looks at their *exteriors*, at their *behavior*, and wants each and every person to be free of judgment, ranking, oppression, domination, coercion, or control by any others. Now unfortunately, what it does not do is take into account the *interior* realities of each of those individuals, and see which of those individuals are actually *in favor of that goal of equality*. Because as it turns out, the *majority* of individuals are *not* in favor of that worldcentric goal. (We saw, according to research, that some 3 out of 5 people are at ethnocentric or lower levels of central identity.) Individuals at crimson archaic and red magic and amber mythic—in short, egocentric and ethnocentric—do not want everybody to be treated equally, to be treated the same. Rather, they want themselves or their special group to have special privileges—because they deserve it, they are the "chosen people"!—and if they are in power at all, they will see to it that their group gets the bulk of the available goods. They will often do so by instigating all manner of coercive and domineering controls—racist, or sexist, or privileged-group favoring, or minority-group devaluing, or allocating the means of production to the favored few, or reserving the bulk of the production capacity for the favored group. But all of those coercive exterior moves are largely driven by an *interior* level of development that is at ethnocentric or lower. (Somebody at worldcentric or higher, on the other hand, will be inherently against any and all such unfair coercive actions, and historically these were the individuals who led or joined the various liberation movements that have resulted in a present-day world where equal rights are unfathomably beyond what any previous epochs of human evolution managed to achieve, or even imagine.)

But green (ignoring interior realities altogether and focusing solely on exteriors) looks at the oppressive actions of the above individuals, and simply attempts to outlaw, criminalize, or behaviorally interrupt those actions. It has no understanding of the actual source and cause of those ethnocentric actions in the first place, no real understanding of the cause of the oppression to begin with. And what is especially crucial to understand in this regard is that, even though culture's center of gravity has moved upward over the millennia from magic egocentric and mythic ethnocentric waves into genuine worldcentric orange and green capacities, everybody today is still *born at square one* and must begin their growth and development from there—and they can *stop* when they reach any of those 6-to-8 stages! And thus even worldcentric cultures everywhere continue to possess individuals at, for example, deeply ethnocentric stages of development—and those individuals possess powerfully oppressive, coercive, and domineering impulses. And thus, among innumerable other fallout items from this disturbing reality, some 200 years since slavery was outlawed, over 50 million people each year are enslaved and trafficked.

Human beings are not born at a worldcentric level of morality, values, or drives—they are not born democratically enthused. They develop to those levels after five or six major stages of development, and by no means does everybody make it. As we've seen, some 60 percent of this culture (and some 70 percent of the world's population) remains at amber ethnocentric (or lower). Every time somebody is making love they are making little Nazis and KKKers to be. The root of such oppressive forces are not caused by exteriors—these specific oppressive forces are not caused by economic factors, nor technological currents, nor political factions, nor geographical realities (although all of those can and do play a contributing role)—but in themselves they are caused by interior realities that have every bit as much existence as any of those exterior occasions.

These interior levels always begin their growth and development from where they were born—with mere physiological drives, wants, and narcissistic needs that can't even take the role of other ("archaic" and "egocentric"). For example, take a child, age 3, and put a ball between you and the child, a ball that is colored red on one side and green on the other—and then spin it several times, so the child can clearly see it is colored differently on each side. Then place the red side toward the child and the green side toward you, and ask, "What color are *you* seeing?" The child will correctly say, "Red." Then ask, "What color am *I* seeing?" And the child will say, "Red." The child cannot take your point of view; the child imagines that what it is seeing is exactly what you are seeing, too. But wait until the child is 7 years old, and then repeat this experiment. This time, ask the child what color it is seeing, and it will correctly say, "Red." Then ask it what color *you* are seeing, and it will correctly say, "Green." What's different is that the child's capacity to take more perspectives has grown, and so it has progressed to a point where it can truly "take the role of other"—it can really put itself in your place and see that you have a different perspective than it does. So as loving as the child most certainly appeared on occasions prior to age 7 or so, it still couldn't see you as an individual; it couldn't realize that you had your own different and separate goals and desires and viewpoints and opinions. It couldn't really see you, and somebody who can't really see you can't truly love you. Or, earlier there is a certain kind of narcissistic love for sure, but now, at this higher stage, when the child says, "I love you," it refers to a much deeper, more authentic love than when it couldn't even see your individual perspective at all, couldn't see you as a real person.

At that previous time, the child wasn't oppressing its love for you—love just had not really had a chance to emerge in an authentic fashion until this point in its growth. The child was still at a "selfish" stage of development, where it saw, and therefore deeply cared for, only itself—it had not yet grown to a "care" stage, where it actually sees, and therefore really cares for, an "other." But now it can take a 2nd-person perspective, and thus really see a 2nd person—such as you—and therefore really love and care for that other person as well. It's not that a repressive force was previously preventing the child from doing this, but simply that the capacity to do this had not yet emerged at all, and so of course the child lacked it. At the selfish stages, care is not being repressed or oppressed; it simply hasn't even emerged yet. This lack is due not to oppression, but to lack of development.

So the individual at this point has developed from being able to entertain only a 1st-person perspective (we saw that as "egocentric"), and now the individual can entertain a 2nd-person perspective (which we saw as "ethnocentric"). Now this individual can expand their identity from just themselves to identifying with a whole group of people (family, tribe, nation, religious group, etc.). If they remain at this general stage, then they will remain primarily identified with their chosen, special group (race or sex or nationality or religion or creed). If, on the other hand, they continue their growth and development and move on to the next major stage, then an even-higher perspective emerges—that of 3rd person, or the capacity to see universal, objective, verifiable realities (often called a scientific capacity, and which we saw as "worldcentric" or *universal* care). Here, a person identifies not just, or not exclusively, with only a single group (race, creed, belief), but now shares a sympathetic identity with all groups, all humans. Because of their universal or worldcentric capacities for perspective, they therefore attempt to treat all people fairly, regardless of race, color, sex, or creed. And it is at this point where the person becomes almost obsessed with freeing any slaves, or releasing anybody from any oppression and unfair subjugation that they might be suffering, or freeing the "untouchables," or making sure genders get the same pay for the same work, or that somebody isn't attacked just for their sexual orientation—a worldcentric, postconventional, universal-care morality.

A person at the previous (ethnocentric) stage does not have this burning drive. It's not because they have no love or care or compassion. They have care (for their chosen group), just not *universal* care (for *all* groups). They love their families deeply; they love their nation passionately; they love their religion dearly. It's simply that their love can only reach up to the special groups that they are identified with—it can't reach to all groups, not yet anyway, no matter how hard the person may try. The mind has to grow and develop its capacity to identify with larger and larger and larger wholes—it is certainly not born identified with all of humanity—and thus it moves from an identity with just "me" (or selfish) to an identity with "us" (or care) to an identity with "all of us" (or universal care). Its inclusivity just keeps getting bigger and bigger and bigger, and therefore more and more people are included in the sphere of its morality and its ethical care. When you are identified with somebody, then you will treat them with care and concern and moral embrace; you will treat them essentially the same way you treat yourself (i.e., you "love your neighbor as you love yourself"). But when you are not identified with them, when they are "other"—they are strange, odd, they don't really fit in, don't really deserve moral embrace—in the worst cases, they might even deserve to be attacked or killed, simply because they are different, they are other, they are not identified with.

As we have been saying, the capacity to identify with others is definitely not gained all at once or from the start. The mind has to increase its capacity for inclusiveness through a slow and arduous growth process, and thus this capacity gets a little bigger (moving from egocentric to ethnocentric—from "me" to "us"), then a little bigger (from ethnocentric to worldcentric—from "us" to "all of us"), and a little bigger still (from worldcentric to integral, which starts to include even other species, resulting eventually in a "cosmic consciousness"—from "all of us" to "all of reality").

This capacity, and its getting progressively bigger and bigger, is just like the mind's being able to write only letters, then words, then sentences, then paragraphs—which it learns to do in that order. It can in no way go from letters to sentences and skip words. And when it is just a word, it cannot be a sentence—these stages can only occur one stage at a time, and none of them can be skipped or bypassed. It's the same everywhere in nature, as with the growth holarchy we've already mentioned: quarks to atoms to molecules to cells to organisms—a stage at a time, none can be skipped, none can be bypassed.

Individuals at a 2nd-person ethnocentric stage have not yet developed the cognitive capacity to think clearly in 3rd-person terms, or in universal or worldcentric terms (they've gone from letters to words, but don't yet have whole sentences), so what remains truly important to them are the ethnocentric identities that they have already formed—a love of family, of country, of their God. But all of those entities are definitely different from the ones that other people elsewhere have (this family versus that family, this country versus that country, this God versus that God). And thus, out of an understandable love for their own cherished identities, they often have a fear, or anger, or even hatred of these "others" who seem to threaten their own kind. And in a sense they do threaten them; but once their awareness and identity has yet again grown and expanded from a 2nd-person ethnocentric turf to 3rd-person worldcentric turf, they won't have any choice but to fight for the realities and goodness of their new territory—which is now a genuinely global or all-inclusive village. They can and will still love their own kind; but their capacity for love has grown enormously, and there are now an extraordinary number of human beings who are genuinely cared about. And so at this point they will deeply and genuinely feel, paraphrasing Kant, that when somebody anywhere suffers, I suffer. And they can't help but feel that—it's not a choice. Thus the emergence of the worldcentric and cosmopolitan stages.

When they themselves were at their previous ethnocentric stage, it is not that they were repressing or oppressing their own global love, postconventional desires, or worldcentric capacities. They simply did not fully see them; they did not yet have that higher-level global capacity—it had not yet truly emerged, nor did they at all identify with it (and not being able to clearly see it, they might even deny its existence, which often happens with things like global warming, which up to half of ethnocentric stages deny even exists—and it's not the "warming" part that they are denying, it's the 3rd-person global worldcentric realities that they cannot clearly see). Thus, at that point, they had no choice but to protect the territory that they could see and that they did identify with—and that was their own family, their own nation, their own God, and very probably their own race, their own sex, their own language. They were indeed very ethnocentric—but not as an oppression of worldcentric realities! They did not see worldcentric realities; for all they knew, they didn't exist. All they saw were things that threatened the realities that they did see—namely, their ethnocentric realities—their families, their jobs, their nations and their borders, their God, their kind.

Of course, there was a time when they did not see those realities either—and that time was, for example, when the green side of the ball was facing the other person and they thought that person was seeing red just like they were. At those selfish stages, the only territory they really saw then was their own—their own egocentric realities, their immediate desires and gratifications, their own wants. But as they continued to grow and evolve, they slowly expanded beyond their limited self-boundaries, and began to identify with all sorts of other people who were in the groups that they began to affiliate with. And this was an enormous expansion for them—an expansion from "me" to "us," an expansion in degrees of freedom, an expansion in the amount of love that they could extend to others, an expansion in the number and types of friends they could have, and on and on—the expansion from egocentric to ethnocentric.

Having done that, what they still could not see, and did not see, was the yet even-greater expansion that a move from ethnocentric to worldcentric, from mythic to rational, from amber to orange, from 2nd person to 3rd person, from local to global, would bring. Oh, they might have been able to think from that orange level (and most of them could indeed do that, could think very rationally from orange), but if they were still *identified* with amber, then they had not yet shifted their own central identity from amber to orange. Their basic identity remained at amber—at ethnocentric, special-group favoring, special-religion favoring, special-culture favoring, maybe special-sex favoring or special-race favoring, even special terrorist-group favoring, and so on almost endlessly.

(And yes, over 90 percent of terrorist groups in the past three decades have had a very strong, amber, ethnocentric central identity—usually with a red-power underbelly—an amber that is almost always of a fundamentalist mythic-literal religious variety, and they see the worldcentric West as "the great Satan," since it certainly is "other" in religious terms, full of infidels and apostates who have no souls—literally—and thus need to be dispatched entirely in the name of the one and only God. And this is an inherent possibility, not merely with extreme Islamic fundamentalists—although statistically there is a significantly higher percentage of those—but with extreme amber fundamentalists in general—whether Southern Baptists blowing up abortion clinics in the South, Buddhists putting poison sarin gas in the Tokyo subway system, Pakistani Muslim and Indian Hindu border warfare, or Catholic and Protestant atrocities in Northern Ireland. Again, the deeper problem isn't with Islamic extremists, it's with amber extremists.)

And what an adult at those stages will do, depending on

numerous other factors, is decide just how much of a threat the other ethnocentric groups themselves are to its own existence, and instead of working to drive all of them upward vertically to the next-higher and more-inclusive level of worldcentric development—where a genuine tolerance and even mutual love between groups and people becomes possible—they might very well decide instead to work only horizontally to strengthen their special group and undercut or even destroy any threatening other groups, whether those might be other professional groups, other nations, other military groups, other races, sexes, economic classes, towns or states, educational levels, economic classes, competitive business products, and so on ad infinitum.

Each of the major basic developmental levels (all 6-to-8 of them)—like all the other holons anywhere in nature—"transcends and includes" its predecessor. This means that each of these levels—as a well-established habit of nature (or "Kosmic groove")—remains available to each person no matter how high they might develop. And when things get very severe, this sequence tends to unravel and regress following exactly the same path and the very same steps, although this time in the reverse direction (downward, not upward). It had evolved from egocentric to ethnocentric to worldcentric to integral, and it will regress from integral to worldcentric to ethnocentric to egocentric. And that is exactly part of the trend that is now in play today, a trend that, we have seen, is partially to credit (or to blame, take your pick) for putting Trump into office. As stress undoes development, integral will tend to slip down into orange or green worldcentric, and worry only about a universal solidarity and not about how to actually integrate all the different levels together in a real holarchical embrace. And the worldcentric levels will slip into ethnocentric, as, for example, green's identity politics slide into incredibly intense racist and sexist embraces—a regression that, in so many areas, we especially saw with green as its original "true but partial" ideas became rigid absolutisms that thoroughly activated amber. And if regression continues, it's no longer even "Save my country, save my religion, save my family!" but "Everybody for themselves!" as primitive egocentrism and narcissism rules the day (and narcissism is so deadly because it undoes any social group entirely; a true narcissist can't even make it up to street gangs).

My simple and central point, after all that digression, is just this: these interior paths can't be intelligently addressed, navigated, and guided if they are simply denied altogether. Whether we're tracing them as they move up to higher and higher levels, becoming more diversity-inclusive, more unified, more loving and caring, or whether they run downhill, becoming more domineering and absolutistic, as they will tend to do whenever societal stress explodes and cultural evolution tends to stall (which is exactly what broken green has given us)—but whether one (or even both) of those occur, they cannot be followed, adequately tracked, and adjusted and guided with any real intelligence or wisdom if we completely deny that they exist in the first place. But that is exactly the profoundly broken ground on which we now stand. Not only America but the world itself (economics to technology to every environmental issue) has been hung out to dry by a broken leading-edge that not only is ignorant of these incredibly important interior currents, but actively attacks and tries to deconstruct them wherever they show up.

Unfortunately, for the past several decades, green has indeed succeeded in exactly that deconstruction. Green's fundamental background belief—its profound aperspectival madness—a demand that all values be seen as "equal" and a categorical refusal to "judge" or "rank" any value system as "better" or "higher"— doesn't allow it to even recognize the grand developmental scale of increasing inclusiveness and increasing care, as well as decreasing oppression and decreasing domination. Should it actually do so, this would immediately allow it to help guide a culture into truly worldcentric and integral realms of reality, where a genuinely free and equal society could actually come into existence.

Green has a correct (and very high) goal of all-inclusiveness, but it doesn't have a single path that actually works to get us there, nor can it truly address the real barriers to its fervently desired ideals. And as it increasingly turned its aperspectival madness on more and more areas—deconstructing more and more aspects of reality—it eventually turned its deconstructive laser on its own existence, deconstructed its own tenets, dissolved any reason to believe anything it had to say, and hence thoroughly collapsed as a functioning leading-edge of evolution.

Hence the urgent question: where do we go from here?

PART THREE

The Immediate Future

7 : Where Do We Go from Here?

The crucial issue at this time is: what do we do next? How can evolution, which has taken a deliberate pause in its ongoing dynamics in order to refurbish its foundations much more adequately and accurately, effectively move forward from what appears on the surface to be such a complete meltdown (most visibly, but by no means solely, represented by Trump's election)?

There are steps that need to be taken at every major level of development (indeed, with every major element in the AQAL matrix), but here we are examining the *major driver* of this meltdown, which is the deconstructive collapse of the green leading-edge in a self-corrective readjustment attempting to find a sturdier base for an ongoing self-organization through self-transcendence (or for transcending and including all previous stages).

With regard to the dysfunctional green leading-edge itself— the actual primary source of the problem (in addition to hundreds of secondary sources)—there are two major possible ways forward, each of which has some hope for alleviating the traffic jam at the leading-edge. The first is the more likely and the less effective, and that involves the healing of the broken and dysfunctional green leading-edge itself—a move of green, by green, on green, aimed at self-healing and self-correction. Amber and orange are each attempting to do more or less what they are supposed to be doing, operating within the (often grave) limitations of their own levels (although both are also suffering, not only from deficits at their own levels, but also from excessive intrusion by a broken green, and that categorically needs to be remedied as part of the green healing). But green, we have seen, has gone off the deep end. In its intense aperspectival madness, it has heightened and inflamed its own malady and inflicted that illness on every area of society that it possibly can. The primary symptom of this is a widespread negative judgment and condemnation of anything amber and orange (anything not green). Green shows no understanding of how and why each of those levels of being and awareness is a necessary stage in a human's overall growth and development—that is, that a person arrives at green itself only because they have first developed through amber and then orange . . . and then green. No amber, no orange—no green. Do you see the suicidal insanity of green hating amber and orange?

Again, for green, these two large blocks (of amber and orange, which are usually mushed together, since green has no conception of individual stages of development) are the great source of the oppressive forces that are turning green people everywhere into "victims," and it tries to crush these forces out of existence with everything from aggressive political correctness, to criminalizing every "micro-aggression" imaginable, to turning every square inch of the country into an ethnocentric-enhancing "safe space," to confusing necessary differentiation with oppression. (Green feels that any "differences" that are recognized between any groups automatically become the source of discrimination and oppression, and thus no differences should be acknowledged in the first place—they are only "social constructions" anyway. And it's true, some are; but some aren't, and this move only imagines more victims everywhere. Green doesn't blame the victim, but it too often creates them.)

The sane action in response to a Trump presidency is exactly an opening between, and a deliberately more friendly embrace between, each of the major stages of development found in all adults. This is a call for a genuine inclusion, not green's version of "inclusion," which is to aggressively exclude everything not green (all of which is seen as a deplorable). Green wants to be inclusive; it theoretically condemns all marginalization, and some of its advocates even call it "the integral culture." But green in fact hates orange, and it hates amber, and it doubly hates 2nd-tier integral (because integral reintroduces healthy versions of all the things that green fought against, including healthy growth holarchies, which green considers the core of domination because it thoroughly confuses dominator hierarchies with growth hierarchies—a distinction discovered and healed by integral).

But right now we are considering the possibility that green can itself heal and reconfigure, and thus resume its role as a truly *leading* leading-edge of evolution (a healing that will almost certainly include many truly integral ideas, but without actually transforming to 2nd-tier integral itself—which is the second major option we will examine in a moment).

The well-known pollster Frank Luntz said, "This [Trump win] is a wake-up call for everyone at every level of government. Governors, Senators, mayors—everyone needs to have a retreat where they can work together to bring about peace in the populace. Importantly, this isn't about government officials reconciling with each another—which in itself is needed. Rather, it is about them facilitating their constituencies to reconcile with each another. It's about bringing people together, bridging our divides and binding our wounds. That's what real leadership is about."

Indeed, in addition to defining an effective education, a primary task of what a leading-edge must do is to provide actual *leadership*. Especially in a world of aperspectival madness (where there is no truth and thus no actual basis for any genuine leadership at all), it can be leadership alone (countering the prevailing go-nowhere currents) that provides an actual way forward—real leadership stares into the face of a no-truth, no-direction, no-values world, and says, "It is simply not true that there is no truth; there is most definitely truth, and it lies in *this* direction"—and it is so radiantly genuine and attractive as it provides a believable path into an uncertain future, that it galvanizes vast numbers to follow it forward.

And at this point in evolution and development, leadership, in order to be truly effective and based on a genuine reality, must take into account the "true but partial" truths of postmodernism itself (as it also must do with traditionalism and modernism)— *but it must do so in their moderate, effective, originally non-extreme and noncontradictory forms,* which originally included genuinely effective means of increasing perspectives and decreasing marginalization. Indeed, and to expand this point across the board, green can truly heal only by deeply befriending the now widely fragmented value systems (especially the three primary ones— traditional amber, modern orange, and postmodern green itself but in a now-healthy form—because these all are at present angrily, even viciously, involved in culture wars gone totally nuclear). Only with such a fundamentally compassionate outreach that sincerely embraces each of those, with a genuine goodwill in place of deep loathing, can green truly heal and thus can the leading-edge once again genuinely begin to function as a real guidance system for effective self-organization.

Much more on that as we proceed. Let me at this point provide a very brief sidebar with a quick sketch of how the three central theoretical tenets of postmodernism—namely, contextualism, constructivism, and aperspectivism, each one of which started as an important "true but partial" concept and was then taken to extremes that directly contributed to the performative contradiction that landed us with aperspectival madness and its tag team of nihilism and narcissism—how each of those can be relocated in their more moderate, effective, noncontradictory, and "true but partial" forms. These more adequate forms can, and indeed should, be fully embraced as a central part of the present dysfunctional green's healing and its return to a more healthy and functional stance. The point is that, as a part of the overall requirement that green compassionately embrace each of the major stages of human development (amber, orange, and green), it must start with its own green values—but values that simply must be cleansed of their extreme, self-contradictory, viciously deconstructive forms. After all, green cannot change the deep features of its own structure—it has to be able to live with itself. All it can do is embrace its healthier, more functional forms and let go of its broken, extreme, even pathological deviations. This is something that green will have to do in any event, even if it just wants to organize and guide its own actions (and not try to embrace other value systems in a larger compassion). If green can't get its own house in order—which has right now almost totally fallen apart—then it is not moving forward for anybody, not others and, most centrally, not itself.

But it will have to do that before it can effectively move on to embracing the amber and orange systems previously so utterly despised by an unhealthy green. So after a quick academic tour of this issue, I'll move directly into stating what this means in plain English. If you're not fond of theoretical excursions, please bear with me; you don't need to remember any of this, and I promise I'll make this section as short as possible.

Here are the three major tenets of postmodernism, and a quick summary of how they can be embraced in their healthier versions (and thus be transcended AND included):

Contextualism: There are no universal truths; all truth is context dependent.

All truth is indeed context dependent, BUT some contexts are themselves universal, and thus universal truth does in fact exist; the very fact that "all truth is contextual" is itself a *universal* context! A diamond will cut a piece of glass, no matter what cultural words we use for "diamond," "cut," and "glass." Stop treating all cross-cultural realities as oppressive and start looking for the many common patterns that connect, which will also point to ways out of an otherwise increasingly fragmented and broken world. (Not to mention that all three major claims of postmodernism that we are now examining are themselves implicitly claimed to be universal truths—and indeed they are.)

Constructivism: All truth is not merely given, it is instead co-constructed.

True, BUT a co-construction nonetheless acknowledged by Wilfrid Sellars as containing various "intrinsic features" that ground the construction. Sellars is the most successful critic of the "myth of the given"—the myth that the world of facts simply exists on its own and by itself, awaiting discovery by all and sundry (postmodernism itself began most fundamentally as a critique of the myth of given, maintaining that reality is instead context dependent and co-constructed, notions that then went extreme). Sellars maintains that there are "intrinsic features" of the world, which provide universalizing grounding—the "co" part of the "co-construction" of knowledge. In short, the "social construction of reality" does not mean "there is no real truth," but it does mean the nature and contexts (from gender to culture) of the knower are an intrinsic part of the knowing process. Further—and most importantly—this opens us to the incredibly sophisticated state of the world when each different genealogical *level of development* will "co-construct" a *different* world (e.g., a red world, an amber world, an orange world, a green world, an integral world, etc.)—something that demands the inclusion of *all* developmental worldviews in any comprehensive knowledge quest.

The general takeaway here is, try and make your co-created world—and thus your leadership—stem from the highest level of development that you can, because each higher level contains not "no truth" but "*more* truth," since each higher stage "transcends and includes" its predecessors. (Not to mention that these three claims of postmodernism are themselves not merely social fabrications or fictions; they are grounded in various "intrinsic features" of the real world that anchor their implicit claims to truth. Integral

Metatheory maintains that these three truths emerge primarily at the green level of evolution and soon become enduring habits and intrinsic features; it is in fact these realities disclosed by green and its perspectives that set the context and help co-construct the truth of these green claims. Yes, these truths are not realized at red or amber, but the higher level disclosing these truths—green—makes the claims not less true but more true—this is what context and co-construction in a genealogical holarchy are all about.)

Aperspectivism: There are no ahistorical, pregiven, privileged perspectives anywhere.

This is the true part of "aperspectivism," and the "partial" part (as in "true but partial") is that each new level of development has been shown to increase the number of perspectives that awareness can take—from a 1st-person perspective of red, to a 2nd-person perspective of amber, to a 3rd-person perspective of orange, to a 4th-person perspective of green, to a 5th-person perspective of early integral, to a 6th-person perspective of late integral, and higher. Each of these stages "transcends and includes" its predecessor, which is the generic drive or Eros of evolution itself, the drive to self-organization through self-transcendence. Thus, no perspective is privileged, because each new emergent stage of evolution produces greater and greater perspective capacity; hence, paraphrasing Hegel, each stage is adequate, each higher stage is more adequate: each stage is true, but each higher stage is "more true," or contains more perspectives that themselves disclose more truths—not *no* facts but *more* facts. This again is why the virtues of a genealogical or evolutionary/developmental view so powerfully offer answers to the aperspectival madness of a chaotic green postmodernism. Thus the "true but partial" truths of postmodernism cannot be denied and hence, like every previous stage, they must be "included"—even as we also dramatically "transcend" them in yet higher integral development of ever-greater and ever-more-inclusive perspectives.

One of the ways that virtually all of postmodernism has been summarized (in addition to "there is no truth, only social constructions") is "there is only history." This is also all of a piece with a "no truth" view, because the extended point is "there is no pregiven, stable truth, because there is nothing but history." With the amber mythic era of human evolution, myths claimed to present "truths" that were eternally or everlastingly real and important, even foundational. "Once upon a time" meant "for all time." As rationality began to emerge, this "forever true" quest was taken up by metaphysics, and the aim of metaphysics—which means, basically, all of Western philosophy—was to provide an account of reality that could be logically proved to be the Last Word on the subject—a presentation of what was "really true" for all time. Something like: "This is the real structure of reality; this is what is true, and this is what is good, and this is what is beautiful; and this account is the one and only really real account of the true nature of the world." The whole point of doing philosophy was to figure it all out, once and for all—the Last Word. No philosopher wrote anything thinking that it would be true for only a year or two and then vanish forever. Metaphysics means finding what is always true, always the Last Word on the subject. And even if they didn't think it was actually possible to do that, it was what virtually all of them wanted.

Until, that is, a little item called "evolution" entered the scene—and the world never recovered. "All that is solid melts into air." Starting with the German Idealists, philosophy became developmental or evolutionary philosophy. It did not assume that reality was a fixed, pregiven, and unchanging set of truths, but rather that reality itself was unfolding, developing, and evolving—and Darwin applied that idea to biology, and Freud to psychology, and Marx to sociology, and the entire ground began to dissolve under us. Modernity began the rethinking of everything in evolutionary terms, and postmodernity took it to its logical conclusion—then beyond, into its illogical extremes, where it crashlanded in nothing but "no truth" land.

The idea was that, starting with the Big Bang, everything that exists went through an evolutionary unfolding, and thus nothing was pregiven or everlastingly true—there was nothing but evolution, "nothing but history." Postmodernist after postmodernist delighted in looking back even just a few hundred years and listing everything that had once been believed in fervently, only to be viewed later as nothing but silly twaddle (and that includes, frankly, pretty much everything humanity has ever believed). Foucault, among many others, gave a "genealogy" (or developmental history) of major beliefs surrounding things like insanity, punishment, evil, sexual mores, and schooling—and delighted in showing their deeply irrational, silly, even mean-spirited origins in addition to showing their virtual incomprehensibility in today's world. One psychiatrist, on reading Foucault's work on the history of madness, said, "If this book is true, our entire profession [of psychiatry] is totally worthless"—there is no dependable truth to it, as its own history so clearly shows. And when there is "only history," there simply is no real truth.

When Thomas Kuhn came out with *The Structure of Scientific Revolutions*, this was all postmodernists needed to finish their argument of "nothing but history" (and hence no real truth anywhere). Kuhn had demonstrated *not* that science is nothing but a conventional social fabrication—as postmodernists everywhere interpreted it—but that science is partially dependent on conventional social practices to move forward (he called these exemplary social practices "paradigms"—by which he did not mean supertheories that invent facts but model practices that help disclose facts). But indeed, postmodernists everywhere took the meaning in its extreme form—that is, that Kuhn had demonstrated that science does not discover enduring truths, but simply discovers "nothing but history" (and thus nothing but historical fabrications). This meant science itself was just one conventional interpretation among many others (it was merely based on assumed, not discovered, "paradigms"), and it had no way whatsoever to prove that its invented interpretation was any better or to be preferred over any others. Thus, the standard postmodern claim became, very quickly, that there was "no difference between science and poetry," no difference between fact and fiction—in short, there is "no truth." If science itself was not discovering anything like truth, then clearly truth itself simply did not exist. And that was the absolute end of the argument as far as postmodernists were concerned: "no truth" henceforth became indisputable postmodern dogma. (Kuhn himself was so exasperated by this misreading of his work that he actually stopped using the term "paradigm" entirely, replacing it with "exemplar," and he clearly stated, "I am a convinced believer in real scientific progress"—that is, real truth that science progressively uncovers. But the goofy cat was already out of the bag, and henceforth "nothing but history" meant "no truth"—period—for postmodernists everywhere.)

There was, nonetheless, a less extreme, more balanced and judicial view of "nothing but history," and this alternative was always present somewhere, even if just in the background of most postmodernists, certainly including Foucault. Namely, as Charles Peirce (generally regarded as America's greatest philosophical genius) would put it, it's fine if we say there are no "nature's laws"—meaning there are no eternally given, never-changing, rigid laws of the universe—but there are, he said, "nature's habits." That is, even if there is nothing but history, much of history actually involves the repetition of regular patterns that have become habitual, or continually repeat themselves. After all, units like atoms have been in existence, repeating themselves, for over 13 billion years—that's a habit much worse than smoking.

So as we look at human history and see all the earlier ideas and beliefs that were so often held by our ancestors, instead of making them all merely chaotic, random, happenstance occasions of "nothing but history," we can indeed trace their *genealogy*—

actually look at history and look for any repeating patterns. When this is done carefully, as by, for example, somebody like the genius Jean Gebser, we find things like an unfolding sequence of genealogical patterns that remain as habits to this day—namely, the stages Gebser called archaic, magic, mythic, rational, pluralistic, and integral. Indeed, these are the repeating stages that developmental psychologists have empirically found in some cases, operating in over 40 different cultures, including Amazon rain forest tribes, Aboriginal Australians, Indianapolis housewives, and Harvard professors—with no major exceptions in all of these. These stages were the basis of those hundred different developmental models that I mentioned, where you could see the same basic 6-to-8 stages repeated over and over again. None of these violate the principles of "nothing but history," but they do point out that significant portions of history do in fact repeat—"nothing but history and its habits."

These reccurring, dependable, regularly repeating patterns of reality are the subsisting elements (or "intrinsic features") that can indeed ground truth—whether in the human realm or the biological, the physical, the sociological, the technological, the economic, the geographic, and so on. And each of the developmental/historical levels of these habits provides a different context and a different co-construction of a phenomenologically different world, with different realities and different truths, *all of which* have to be taken into account to get a truly comprehensive and accurate overview of truth (which is what we are doing here). This is the real conclusion of "nothing but history and its habits."

Of course, there are also an infinite number of spontaneous, fresh, and nonrepetitive events as well—but none of those, since they don't repeat, can be claimed to be an "enduring truth." And there are also an almost infinite number of new, novel, emergent events, events that are, in whole or part, appearing for the very first time—the "transcend" part of "transcend and include"—and *if* those are repeated, then they are entering the realm of enduring habits, a la Peirce, and thus can begin to ground real truths. Say something that accurately reflects some aspect of this repeating pattern, and you have a legitimate representational truth. (There are other types of validity claims as well, including truthfulness, goodness, and aesthetics, among others, and these simply reflect different dimensions of ongoing, repeating patterns of emergent evolution. In other words, there are ways to redeem all legitimate validity claims. So even with "nothing but history," there are legitimate truth claims. For sure, this massively expands what we mean by "truth." For example, there isn't just sensorimotor truth—there are also red truths, amber truths, orange truths, green truths, turquoise truths, and so forth. And this expanded reality is what makes dealing with things like "fake news" a bit more sophisticated than simply pointing to sensorimotor facts and trying to anchor everything in crude material entities. This simply shows that taking truly "integral" or "comprehensive" approaches to this problem—allowing the partial truths of postmodern contextualism, constructivism, and aperspectivism—is absolutely crucial.)

This approach relieves us from any attempt at a typical metaphysics—it is not looking for the Last Word, but simply the First Word—and yet it also saves us from an extreme postmodernism ("No Word at all!"), which has simply run aground in its own performative contradictions (if "nothing but history" is applied in extreme form, then even that belief itself is only a historical happenstance and cannot claim to be an enduring truth at all—hence, there is no compelling reason to believe it whatsoever, and, as usual, postmodernism deconstructs itself). This whole approach is what we in the Integral movement call "Integral Post-Metaphysics," the whole point of which is that there are indeed ways to accept and embrace the central tenets of postmodernism—contextualism, constructivism, and aperspectivism—without push-

ing them into their extreme deconstructive forms, where they do
nothing but tear down the entire world—including, eventually,
all of their own claims. In other words, we can "transcend and
include" postmodernism, which is exactly what 2nd-tier integral
does in reality.

Which is to say, there is in fact hope—and that's the truth.

8 : Dominator Hierarchies and Growth Hierarchies

Okay, back to the real world. One of the simplest points here is that, for green to move from its extreme, dysfunctional, unhealthy, and pathological condition to a state of healthy, vibrant, true leading-edge capacities, it is absolutely central that green heal its catastrophic confusion between dominator hierarchies and actualization hierarchies. Actualization (or growth) hierarchies are not exclusive and domineering, they are inclusive and integrating. As we saw, in a dominator hierarchy, the higher the level, the more it can oppress and dominate (as with the caste system, or criminal organizations like the Mafia). With growth hierarchies (or "holarchies"), it's *exactly the opposite.* In a growth holarchy, the whole of each level becomes an included part of the whole of the next higher level—just as, in evolution, a whole quark becomes part of an atom, a whole atom becomes part of a molecule, a whole molecule becomes part of a cell, a whole cell becomes part of an organism, and so on. Each level is a whole/part, a "holon." The ever-increasing inclusiveness—genuine inclusiveness—of holons and holarchies demonstrates a direction that is grounded in nature and that has been operative from the first moment of the Big Bang forward, a direction of self-organization through self-transcendence that is the primary drive of evolution itself.

Another way to say "transcend and include" is "differentiate and integrate." Each stage of development differentiates the previous stage, and then integrates those newly emergent parts into a higher-level order (which usually tends to be a very enduring habit). Thus, a single-cell zygote first splits into 2 cells, then 4, then 8, then 16, then 32 (and so on) differentiated cells, and after those are introduced, they are integrated into inclusive systems— a nervous system, a muscular system, a digestive system, and so on—all of which are integrated in the overall organism. Each stage of this growth process goes beyond (or transcends) the previous stage but also includes or enfolds it, and it does so by differentiating and integrating it.

Green's accomplishment was that, by introducing a 4th-person perspective that could reflect on—and hence criticize—the 3rd-person systems of orange (including its many early sciences), green began to differentiate those orange monolithic, static, nonpermeable systems, producing not a single given world system, but a rich multicultural display of an almost limitless variety of differentiated systems. That is the "true" part.

The "partial" part is that, while it could differentiate these many systems, it could not yet integrate them. It saw nothing but a riot of cultural differentiation, and since no holarchy or truly increasing inclusivity or integration could be seen, it simply imagined that all of them are absolutely equal—hence, its "egalitarianism," which really represented its incapacity to find the deeper (or higher) patterns that connect, the integrating holarchies that tie together the various world systems and indeed allow and facilitate their interactions in the first place.

One last little academic point (just this one paragraph). We saw that, of course, green really didn't believe this idea of equality, since it definitely felt that its view of this situation was much better than any view that did not see it this way—its view was superior in a world where nothing was supposed to be superior. So much for "egalitarianism." But it couldn't officially acknowledge that its own view was higher than, for example, orange modern, because it officially denied *all* hierarchies—not just dominator hierarchies, but growth hierarchies as well—hence its performative contradiction of directly expressing a hierarchical view while simultaneously denying all hierarchical views. It would only be with the "monumental leap" to integral 2nd tier that actualization (or growth) holarchies would become a standard and recognized part of the "intrinsic features" of the real world. This inherent recognition of growth holarchies was, in other words, a "turquoise truth"—a truth emerging for the first time only at the turquoise integral level—and thus something that a green news agency, for example, *would not be able to accurately report*, try as it may. Hence, the real delicacy of deciding just what is "fake news" in a holarchical world of genealogical levels, where each higher level sees "more truths"—and truths that *cannot be seen* by lower levels, so how would those levels accurately report higher truths and higher news? How could a green news agency accurately report turquoise truths? And the answer is, it can't—which is why, as only one example, we have constantly seen that green repeatedly distorts any reporting of hierarchy, claiming it is always domineering and oppressive, when more often it is actualizing and growth enhancing—and there is fake news in action. Turquoise has suffered fake news at the hands of green for decades, and truly mean-spirited "news" at that. Of course, this *also* means that an amber news agency could not accurately see or report green truths—does Fox News come to mind here? But you can see the delicacy of defining "fake news" when, in reality, there are developmental levels of truth and facts (with each higher level marked not by "no truth," but by "more truth"—amber sees more than red; orange sees more than amber; green sees more than orange; turquoise sees more than green—and we have an overwhelming amount of evidence—of facts—demonstrating exactly that). Only by taking *all* holarchical levels of development carefully into account can truly avoiding fake news ever become possible. That, needless to say, is a stunningly complex issue, and one that we are not directly dealing with in this presentation—as I said, I recommend picking up any book on Integral Metatheory for that. Here we are dealing with the much more fundamental and simpler issue of the denial of truth and facts altogether—that is the catastrophe at large that we are addressing. We're focusing on the denial of truth itself, the denial of any facts at all, whether high or low or anywhere in between. That is the disaster of a "post-truth" world, and that is our primary focus.

Back to our narrative. Because the important point is that even green—healthy green—can learn to stop confusing these actualization holarchies with all the truly nasty dominator hierarchies that are out there (even if this is something it has to repeatedly tell itself, over and over). But how hard is it, really, to spot the difference between a dominator hierarchy and a growth hierarchy? Actually, not that hard at all, once it's been really pointed out, but nonetheless, that hasn't stopped green from aggressively denying absolutely every form of holarchical depth (and every type of hierarchy) in existence; hence green has no concept of a genuine direction—for green, no perspective is higher or more inclusive than another, and so no truth is available at all. And with that, the leading-edge has collapsed entirely, viciously crashed by a performative contradiction that landed it in aperspectival madness, which then oversaw a world becoming more and more slightly mad. Introducing growth holarchies—in literally all areas where real growth and development is occurring (which is most of them)—would allow green to take up, once again, some actual conception of what *direction* means: not only a horizontal increase in *aptitudes* for all, but a vertical increase in *altitude* for all.

And there is a truly simple reason that the introduction of growth holarchies is so crucial for any effective path forward. Green is rightly concerned about dominator hierarchies, but research makes it unbelievably clear that the only people who engage in dominator hierarchies are those who are at the very lowest levels of growth hierarchies. Only someone at Gilligan's selfish (egocentric) or special-group care (ethnocentric) will even want to dominate and oppress in the first place. And correlatively, those who criticize and reject dominator hierarchies (and historically fought for their destruction) are those at the truly higher levels of growth hierarchies (orange, green, and integral). At Gilligan's universal care (or worldcentric), you care for ALL people, regardless of race, color, sex, or creed (even more so at integral). Thus, when green rejects *all* hierarchies (dominator and growth), it manages to accurately spot the problem but also, in the very same step, to completely destroy the cure.

In short, green's fake news about hierarchies in general destroys not only their truly nasty and domineering forms, but also their genuine growth and actualization forms as well. This is a cultural disaster of the first magnitude—blame for which lies squarely on broken green's doorstep.

Thus we have one of the greatest, most widespread, most damaging disasters handed to us by aperspectival madness. When green in general—social warriors, marginalization liberators, feminists of many varieties, overall liberalism, nongovernmental organizations (NGOs) everywhere—stormed into any area and began an aggressive "Down with all hierarchy!" many cases of cultural oppression were, at least to begin with, upended and deconstructed—along with every truly effective means of growth to rebuild the oppressed area. By killing all growth holarchies, green killed all growth. (That is, it removed the morphogenetic background of increasing interior growth and development, and was left with nothing but a vacuous assertion of "specialness" for all the marginalized groups. But simply asserting, over and over, "I am special, I am special" does precisely nothing to end the real source of the oppressive force—another catastrophic failure of the leading-edge.)

And it was by no means, in any way, just the marginalized groups that needed the means of truly transformative growth processes to be made available to them; the entire force drivers of oppression especially needed to be exposed to effective means to open themselves to continued growth, from egocentric to ethnocentric to worldcentric to integral (via any of literally hundreds of growth techniques, exercises, and practices demonstrated to accelerate interior growth and evolution). Instead of approaching the actual source of the oppressive drive—that is, the interior (or Left-Hand) dimensions of arrested development—green attacked the symptoms—that is, the exterior (or Right-Hand) behavior of the oppressors—which does nothing to uproot the real problem but simply sends it underground to morph and regenerate and pop up elsewhere. (Clearly, any truly effective approach will attack oppression as it manifests in all 4 quadrants, as well as all levels—that is, AQAL. But to utterly leave out half of the conditions—and the most important half at that, the very source and cause of the interior drive itself—is to end up being, sooner or later, outstandingly ineffective.)

We talked earlier about the real problems that come from looking just at exteriors and not also taking interiors into account, especially when we are looking at things like oppression, us-versus-them viciousness, hate crime, and any sort of racist, sexist, homophobic, xenophobic beliefs. This is true for any level of development, but we're especially talking about green right now, so let me give an example using that. Let's say that green activists are looking at 100 people brought together in a town meeting, and they want them to express views that genuinely embrace diversity and inclusiveness. So green gives courses and lectures and workshops on how to behave in ways that reflect real equality, replete with teachings about trigger warnings, safe spaces, and microaggression. The green activists tell the crowd that, yes, it might take some of them a bit of learning, but "we'll be watching you, and chastise any behavior that isn't appropriate, and soon enough you'll learn." Variations on that approach can be found among any social justice activists anywhere.

It's not that such approaches are totally wrong; they're just mostly wrong. Or, at any rate, they are mostly incomplete. Let's now view this situation by not just looking at 100 bodies and watching their exterior behavior carefully; let's also look at their interiors and take those into account. Using Robert Kegan's research, we saw that, on average, 3 out of 5 Americans are at ethnocentric or lower stages of development. That means, out of this crowd of 100 people, fully 60 of them are at ethnocentric or lower. And that means that those 60 individuals, in reality, want nothing to do with equality. They do not want to treat all people fairly regardless of race, color, sex, or creed. In fact, they have some sort of deep ethnocentric beliefs—they could be racist, or sexist, or fundamentalist religious, or politically zealous, or extreme white supremacist or extreme feminist or scientician or extreme patriot. They want special treatment for their special group, and they will fight any efforts to extend those same treatments to all people. If they truly get caught and punished for behavior indicative of these beliefs, they will quickly learn to disguise those beliefs by changing their behavior—while in the meantime continuing to embrace those ethnocentric beliefs with renewed vigor.

Yet all of that goes completely over the heads of the green activists. They can see none of it; what's worse, they are looking for none of it, because they are largely ignorant of these interior stages of development themselves (and they are ignorant of them because, for the most part, they have confused these growth holarchies with dominator hierarchies and already thoroughly condemned all of them outright).

And thus, 40 of these 100 people will largely resonate with these social justice activists, yet 60 of the 100 will do nothing of the sort, but rather renew secretly their ethnocentric commitments and zealous beliefs, while developing an intense and widespread ressentiment at those elites trying to "educate" them. The more the "elites" try, the deeper the ressentiment grows. This goes nowhere extremely fast, and coupled with the native loathing of ethnocentric individuals by the green pluralists, the situation soon ends up with half of the crowd thoroughly hating the other half, a hatred that is deeply mutual.

So, if we are green activists and we want to embrace "diversity" and we want to be "completely all-inclusive," then does that mean, out of these 100, that we give an *equal voice* to the 60 racists? An equal voice to the 60 sexists? An equal voice to any Nazis or KKKers or rabid fascists? You see the fundamental problem here? If by "diversity" and "inclusivity" we simply mean a body count, an equal voice and equal value and equal inclusivity for absolutely everybody who simply shows up—without any awareness or care about whether they themselves also actually want diversity and inclusivity, or instead actually want to deny and deeply undermine diversity and inclusivity—if we are emphasizing those voices equally, then clearly we are headed for a great deal of trouble. We won't even be able to check on the worldcentric activists to see whether they start regressing into ethnocentric fundamentalisms (which too many green have done in the past few decades with, for example, the ethnocentric-enhancing identity politics). If whenever you say "diversity" and "inclusiveness," you mean "let's be sure and include the Nazis and the KKK," then just keep doing exactly what you are already doing. Keep tracking only exteriors and completely ignore interiors, and in no time we will have a society that fully values and includes racists and sexists and all manner of egocentric and ethnocentric exclusivities.

As it turns out, what we do in a democracy is give each exterior body one vote (unless they have actually behaved criminally), and I am in no way advocating that we stop doing that (one person, one vote; "nobody is above the law"—and nobody is beneath it, either). But I *am* advocating that we stop completely ignoring these interior realities. At the very least, we want to take these interiors into account in our educational systems, and look to genuinely help individuals grow, evolve, and develop from their egocentric to their ethnocentric to their worldcentric to their integral possibilities—not simply point to all 100 people and count them equal when it comes to law and democracy, but also remember to look at their interiors when it comes to what we applaud and champion in this culture. If we simply look at the 100 and say, "Let's equally include them all with no further ado," then we are equally including 60 people who categorically do not want to include the others. At some point, that badly and deeply backfires, and severely undercuts our own deepest wishes and highest ideals. (In fact, with a democracy, this results directly in what James Madison called "the tyranny of the majority." If 60 percent of the population is ethnocentric, then democracy will happily vote Trump. Hitler, in fact, was democratically elected.)

This also explains the complete traffic jam in exactly what social justice activists actually do champion. Officially, they maintain that they want "total diversity" and "complete inclusiveness." And yet in their protests, they loudly condemn (and scream at) any obvious racists, sexists, homophobes, and so forth. Their official stance is that there are no superior views—that "what's true for you is true for you, and what's true for me is true for me." But clearly, they do not believe that. They categorically do NOT believe that "what's true for you is true for you, and what's true for me is true for me"—if they did believe that, why are they yelling so loud at racists and sexists, who have their own "true for them" truths?

These green activists are doing so because in fact they have a value hierarchy—at its best, not a dominator hierarchy but a genuine growth hierarchy, which places worldcentric inclusivity above ethnocentric oppression and exclusion. And yet, again, officially, they deny all hierarchies and all "nasty ranking" entirely. Everywhere you turn here there is a performative contradiction— they are doing and saying exactly what they maintain you cannot and should not do: namely, deny aperspectival madness and embrace what they clearly believe is a superior view. In this case, they are NOT saying, "What's true for you is true for you, and what's true for me is true for me." They are instead saying, and very loudly, "No, in this case, what's true for me [worldcentric] *better be true for you*, too, you racist [ethnocentric] dude, or we're going to have trouble." And yet nowhere in their belief system can green legitimate that belief, since officially there is only aperspectival madness and a stance of no-truth (no hierarchies, no rankings, no judgments). If even science is no truer than fiction, fat chance these "superior values" have.

You have to realize what a deep, troubled, horridly confused stance a performative contradiction is. It actually and strongly denies any reality to your own existence. When you wholeheartedly announce that "you can't say any values are better than others," that statement itself actually denies that it has any believability (if no beliefs are better than others, that belief itself is no better than any others, and hence there's no real reason to embrace it at all). It doesn't even take two sentences to contradict itself—just that one sentence, and it has completely turned on itself. The statement itself claims to be better than the alternatives, yet that claim of superiority is exactly what it totally denies. Its existence denies its own existence. And the person walking around with such a belief is a walking self-denial machine, a perpetual self-deconstruction device, racked with a deep existential insecurity. This is why, as we've constantly seen, postmodernists who profess such views actually don't believe them—their very embrace of those views is actually a claim that they are in fact true, which is why they have embraced them, and thus they undercut their own beliefs as soon as they open their mouths. But keep in mind, as obvious as this might seem right now, an entire epoch of philosophy and human sciences was avidly devoted to exactly such performative contradictions, resulting in, among numerous other disasters, our present culture of post-truth.

Let's be very clear. From a worldcentric and integral stance, we do indeed want real diversity, we want genuine inclusiveness. But that will take more than someone pointing at all 100 people and simply saying, "We are all one! We all love each other! We make room for everybody! Everybody is welcome! America's arms are wide open to everybody!" It takes more than just pointing at exteriors and emotionally pronouncing them all one. *It takes the interior growth, evolution, and development of each and every person* in that crowd of 100, from their own basest egocentric and narcissistic drives (with which we are all born), through their ethnocentric and exclusivist drives (a phase through which we all grow—and many remain), to their worldcentric and integral possibilities, which represent the deepest wishes and highest ideals (that have evolved to date) of good people everywhere. That interior growth (in consciousness and culture) is the actual *path* to our cherished goals of a real diversity and true inclusivity. Anything less than that yields nothing but nasty versions of less-than-diverse and less-than-inclusive voices, and if those voices are being blindly included in the round table, we will never reach our ideals. What is of concern here is not the ideals or the goals, but *the complete lack of any real interior path to those goals*—and not even the lack of a real path, but the aggressive attacks on any real paths as if they were nothing but "dominator hierarchies"! Talk about suicidal.

So again, it's not that the core beliefs of the green activists are wrong. It's that they are entirely ignorant of the interiors of those whom they are trying to evolve. Of course, they are ignorant of their own developmental interiors as well, which certainly doesn't help. But my point is simply that, for green to re-assume anything like a truly *leading* leading-edge role, it simply must, at the very least, stop confusing growth hierarchies with dominator hierarchies. Even better, of course, would be to admit that interiors are actually real, then study the massive amount of research on these interior stages themselves, and thus truly become expert in devising ways to genuinely help people grow and evolve to ever more inclusive, more diversity-embracing, and more caring and loving levels of development. *Nothing short of that interior development will do anything at all to actually stop ethnocentric oppression and divisiveness.* And at the very least, stop actually attacking and viciously condemning people who are attempting to do this!

One of the paradoxical reasons that it is so important that our culture at large understand the general basics of a developmental view is that such an understanding would allow people to see the general limits to how much they will be able to agree with each other in the first place. All 1st-tier stages (crimson, magenta, red, amber, orange, and green), as we saw, think that their truth and values are the only genuinely real and important truth and values in existence. That is not likely to ever change fundamentally (it hasn't for the last hundred-thousand years that this trait has been in existence). But the degree to which those beliefs are held, and the aggression that is invested in such a belief, can indeed be softened, opened, dosed with a bit of kindness and compassion—and the example for this must come from the leading-edge. That's one of the things that a leading-edge does: while being essentially the "highest" level of evolution at that point, *it leads all levels*—it provides a direction that can energize the population at large—and failing that, it fails to lead. That is exactly one of the problems that the collapse of green ended up generating—all other values were not met with an open compassion but were aggressively "deconstructed" and decommissioned and tossed in the "basket of deplorables," and anyone who continued to believe them was subjected to harsh, vocal, and unrelenting ridicule. The "culture wars" (which, again, are exactly the battles between amber, orange, and green—between traditional mythic religion, modern science and business, and postmodern multiculturalism)—but the culture wars, under green "leadership," went nuclear.

Sadly, what green was actually teaching this culture, by example, were sophisticated ways to despise (and deconstruct) those who disagree with you—they aren't just wrong, they are the source of every major force of oppression, injustice, slavery, and worse. You do not want to embrace them with kindness and understanding, you literally want to deconstruct them (while you yourself flounder in aperspectival madness, cackling loudly with each new victory of helping move others to an equal infestation by aperspectival insanity). What so desperately needs to be understood, from a developmental and evolutionary perspective, is that each major *stage of development* becomes a possible *station in life* for those who stop there, and there is nothing that can be done about that—except to make sure that all the means of further development are made as widely available as possible (a core task of the leading-edge), and—just as importantly—make room in the society for individuals who are at each station of life (red, amber, orange, green, or integral), and douse the whole affair with outrageous amounts of loving kindness—and *do this by example.*

Will green ever again be able to lead by healthy example? Everybody's got a stake in this. Just as, whether Obama is president or whether Trump is, in any case, that's *our* president, like it or not. Similarly, green is our leading-edge, like it or not, and how it takes up that role in the coming years will have a staggeringly huge impact on every one of us. None of us are immune. Thus, in order to fully understand green's chances of actually leading in a competent and flourishing fashion, let's briefly look at any other items that green has denied or deconstructed, and see if there are any other truly central factors that need to be addressed and included.

In short, what else would green need to understand in order to effectively pick up once again a vibrant and radiant role at the leading-edge? And how would that directly impact those who are right now simply "resisting" and "fighting" Trump?

9 : The Lessons Green Must Learn

There have actually been a moderate but noticeable number of green voices that seem to genuinely have gotten the central message. That is to say, I've heard many staunchly green individuals say that the primary lesson they got from this election was not how much they hated Trump and despised his followers (although that is an extremely common, probably majority, response), but that they had to reach out to this huge group of people who put Trump in office—that they had spent their adult lives basically looking down on them, making fun of them and ridiculing them, and what was required instead was to genuinely and truly understand them, to include them in the dialogue, to open themselves to seeing the world from their point of view, to make room for them in their world. And this indeed is exactly the type of genuine healing that embraces the self-correction that evolution is looking for. The leading-edge cannot lead if it despises those whom it is supposed to lead. It cannot go forward one more step if it has no idea of what a true "forward" means (which it can't do if it has no belief in "truth" itself). It cannot move into a greater tomorrow if it denies "greater" and "lesser" (growth holarchies) altogether, and instead sees all values as absolutely equal (which we saw it doesn't really believe anyway, because it definitely believes its values are superior).

What green especially needs to understand is that the capacity to embrace its green values is itself the product of several stages of development or a growth holarchy, and hence—even if it just wants to see more green "diversity" and "inclusiveness" get produced—then it categorically must get behind that genealogy or growth holarchy as a truly valid—and "true"—way to move forward in a pluralistic postmodern world.

This path forward would also involve cleaning out the extreme and broken green elements that have invaded all the other 1st-tier stages (red, amber, orange, and healthy green itself). At green, the whole "aperspectival madness" disease has to be rethought and rejected in its many forms. As we saw in our little academic sidebar, it's true that all knowledge is context-bound (but some contexts are universal, and thus some knowledge is too); and it's true that all knowledge is constructed (but it is co-constructed with subsisting intrinsic factors in the actual world, and thus is not just a "fabrication"); and it's true that no perspective is privileged (which actually means that the more perspectives that you include, the more adequate and more accurate your map becomes). Technologically, the Information Age (the Lower-Right-quadrant social correlate of the Lower-Left-quadrant green wave of cultural development) all too soon became infected with aperspectival madness itself, and, as we saw, it stopped having algorithms that select for the Good, or the True, or the Beautiful, and instead simply feeds back one's own narcissistic tendencies. As *Time* magazine put it, "The Internet's personality has changed. Once it was a geek with lofty ideals about the free flow of information. Now, if you need help improving your upload speeds the web is eager to help with technical details, but if you tell it you're struggling with depression it will try to goad you into killing yourself. Psychologists call this the online disinhibition effect, in which factors like anonymity, invisibility, a lack of authority and not communicating in real time strip away the mores society spent millennia building. And it's seeping from our smartphones into every aspect of our lives." This has gotten so bad it often invites regression beyond ethnocentric to deeply egocentric and narcissistic enthusiasms (and "narcissism" does not mean a healthy and proud self-opinion, it means valuing and promoting oneself at the expense of all others).

The utterly free flow of, and access to, all information is a noble ideal. But it's just that—a value, an ideal. In addition to a free flow of data, indexing capacities that are "envalued"—that deal with items like degree of depth, expanse of perspectives (and thus "amount" of truth), developmental holarchies, and other envalued judgments (such as the Good, the True, the Beautiful)—need to be made as available as supposedly "value free" systems. We saw that Google primarily searches information based on its popularity, so the information it retrieves basically reflects the prejudices of the most number of people. Even offering the option to search for "least popular" in addition to the default "most popular" would be a start. But the ways that the online world actually embeds and transmits very extensive—and very limited—value systems need to be increasingly addressed. When Douglas Rushkoff can write a book entitled *Throwing Rocks at the Google Bus*, you know something's deeply wrong.

In addition to green's simply taking care of itself and healing its extremist, deconstructive, nasty-edged aperspectival madness (by, for instance, expressing its three main tenets in more moderate and healthy forms, and distinguishing between dominator hierarchies and growth holarchies, thus actually finding a direction to establish a real leadership), what measures can a broken green take to repair its invasive damage of the lower stages?

As for orange economics, although the analyses of this would take a book or two to be complete (as it would for any of these factors), we might start with the economic notion of a guaranteed annual income. As we noted, technologically the world is moving toward a truly utopian but real work-free situation, where everybody would, one way or another, be guaranteed to receive all the (material) basics of a life well lived. And the sooner that happens, the better. Yet this will actually take considerable reworking of both economic theories and economic practices. This is so, in part, because a fundamental problem of most present-day economic theories is that they still essentially reflect the scientific materialism of the eighteenth and nineteenth centuries, when they were first created. In short, they track only exterior, material money and wealth, not also interior consciousness and culture. The problem with money is that it can buy almost any artifacts in the Right-Hand quadrants (which are all material or physical items), but it can buy virtually nothing on the interior or Left-Hand quadrants (consciousness, love, care, compassion, intelligence, values, meaning, purpose, vision, motivation, spirituality, emotional goods, mental ideas). Thus, when the gross national product is calculated—which is often taken as an indicator of the overall success of individuals' lives—not a single one of those really important items is taken into account at all, not even remotely. There is now a growing and vocal discontent that points out that present economic indexes don't include things like caregiving or parenting or family/relational realities, or any sort of life values at all (which is really just the beginning of an integral inventory of what they don't include). When we decide that society will provide essentially all the items required for a full life—and we have theories and models and statistics that begin to track all *those* elements—exactly what elements will those be? A broken green is the *last* wave you want trying to answer that.

And as the average human lifespan reaches and then significantly bypasses the century mark, what will humans do when they don't have to work? This is something that every culture is going to have to answer in a truly effective way—or face true disaster. My point again is that aperspectival madness is exactly what you don't want in charge of finding these answers.

(My own view, which I first put forth in the book *Boomeritis*, is that, after humans are provided all the Right-Hand material goods that they want, what is left for them to want—especially when they start living for as long as a century or two? What could they possibly do with all that time? And the answer is, turn their exploration from the mere exterior world into the vast worlds of interior and virtually unlimited horizons, tasting all the goods in the Left-Hand domains. That is, any society able to effectively deal with people living hundreds of years will have to make knowledge of the many interior levels and states of consciousness available, so that people can begin to pursue the incredibly vast and massively different interior worlds provided by the almost limitless vistas of the higher states and stages of being and awareness—and enjoy the staggeringly rich increase in consciousness, bliss, awareness, love, compassion, joy, and happiness that those higher states and stages can bring. These generally begin with the territory of an integral view—which we'll discuss in a moment—but they could start to be made available by a healthy and open green.)

In any event, a small technical item that orange business could use right now is the easing of the massive number of regulations that a hyper-sensitive green has put into place. Small businesses in particular are failing in record numbers, as green's attempts to prevent employee "victims" has virtually paralyzed much of a healthy business operating capacity. This is just a general example of what we're talking about overall here, which is the difference between a healthy green care and a hyper-sensitive green obsession, which, in attempting to remove *all* suffering from *all* life conditions, effectively removes the conditions themselves and, as an unintended consequence, ends up increasing suffering, sometimes enormously (to green's colossal confusion).

The necessity of giving more awareness to the downsides of a hyper-sensitivity run amok certainly applies to extreme political correctness. The orange drive of free speech versus the green drive of equality has come out with too much "transcend" and not enough "include"—individual free speech and wide-open knowledge acquisition has been sunk in favor of group rights and an overall equality that doesn't transcend and include freedom but transcends and trashes it, transcends and denies it, transcends and even criminalizes it. The cure for this—well, this is so obvious I'll just give one example: this problem will have been adequately addressed when the great comedians of our time are again willing to play college campuses. The same goes for microaggression, triggers, and safe spaces—they should be allowed to exist only if they can directly face a freed comedy.

As for the effect of green's aperspectival madness on amber ethnocentric stages, this is the level that truly requires a conscious intention on the part of green, if green wishes at all to heal its nastiness (what Integral theorists, we saw, call "the mean green meme") and become fit, once again, to actually be the leading-edge. This requires not agreeing with amber, not acting on amber, not accepting all of amber's actions, but genuinely reaching out in human understanding, compassion, and kindness (while still holding any amber ethnocentric actions that violate worldcentric well-being accountable with sanctions of one variety or another). And this does involve a genuine softening of the widespread view that amber is intrinsically "deplorable."

Such a view ("they're deplorable") might be admissible if amber's decisions were an actively free choice, but for the most part they aren't: one does not choose one's stage of development or its characteristics; these simply come with the territory of that stage itself, and they will persist—whether you like them or not—until that stage passes. The most we do in a "judgmental" fashion is use developmentally discriminating wisdom to make all means of growth as available as possible, while still sanctioning any overt behavior—racist, sexist, homophobic, misogynistic—coming directly from such ethnocentric stages. But this does not include judging somebody who is actually at an ethnocentric stage as if they voluntarily and gleefully chose those traits as a deliberate moral choice. It's not as if somebody said, "Okay, here's the deal: you are allowed to choose to treat fairly only your own particular group, or you can choose to treat all groups fairly, regardless of race, color, sex, or creed, and whether or not they happen to be your group"—and the person is actually completely free to choose either of those, and then they deliberately say, "Oh, I want to identify just with my special group, and I couldn't give a rat's ass about the rest of humanity." In 9 out of 10 times, that is not what happens. The ethnocentrically biased person is not open to that type of complex choice; they are not coming from a worldcentric space and then deliberately choosing a prejudiced ethnocentric stance (if they did that, they would indeed be truly "deplorable"). Rather, for the most part, they are coming from an egocentric stance and are just moving up to an expanded care, embracing not just themselves but an entire group of people—they are moving from "selfish" to "care" (on the way to "universal care" and "integrated")—a real move up.

For such an individual, our appropriate response is to feel not a gloating moral superiority, but a truly deep compassion for someone living within the unbelievably constricting, suffocating, and suffering-inducing stages that these are—and from an integral view, *compassion* is the only judgmental attitude we're allowed—the *only* one.

But it is precisely a lack of compassion, care, and understanding that broken green has avidly displayed (in academia, media, entertainment, and liberal politics). And more than any other single item, this mean-green-meme attitude is what caused the huge reservoir of ressentiment that led to Trump's previously unimaginable win. A full 81 percent of those who described themselves as "angry" voted for Trump. 8 out of 10! That is by far the highest percentage demographic group going for Trump—much more than white, or male, or undereducated, or underclass—*angry*. And who are they angry at? Well, I hate to say it, but probably you.

(Okay, maybe me, too—us. The point is, it's fully 50 percent of the country angry at the other 50 percent, so take your pick—and that fact, as we've often noted, is something that *cannot* continue, or this country will literally break in half.)

Finally, as I said, much of egocentric speaks for itself. I'll simply add the idea that I introduced with the notion of "boomeritis." In the book by that title, I point out that, although the Boomers were indeed known as the "Me generation" and the "culture of Narcissism," they weren't just a generation of kids characterized by narcissism per se. Rather, the Boomer generation had a very high level of development that was infected with a very low level of development. It was green pluralism infected with red narcissism/egocentrism. It was a condition—marked primarily by the Boomer generation, hence its name the "Me generation," but not a condition by any means confined to the Boomers—that is the result of an extensive "pre/post fallacy." This fallacy occurs because both PRE-conventional realities (such as egocentrism) and POST-conventional realities (such as autonomy and individualism) are both fully NON-conventional, and thus they are easily and often confused and equated. Either pre-conventional realities are *elevated* to post-conventional truths (so that narcissistic and egocentric stances are taken to be very high expressions of fully autonomous individuality), or else post-conventional realities are *reduced* to pre-conventional childish modes (so that nonconformist postconventional individuals are charged with being narcissistic and self-promoting). "Boomeritis" is a variety of the former, or elevationism, where—precisely due to the pluralistic/relativistic stance of aperspectival madness—all stances were taken to be equally acceptable, and thus a very low narcissism could hide out in a very high autonomous individualism.

We see examples of this, for instance, in some of the Vietnam War protests. In one Berkeley protest, the students claimed in one voice that their objections to the war were based on universal moral principles—the war was morally wrong, and thus it should be protested against—and yet tests of the moral development of the protesters showed that, while a few of them were indeed at universal postconventional (or worldcentric) stages of moral development, a large majority of them—over 70 percent—were actually at the pre-conventional, egocentric stages of moral development (they didn't want the war, not because it was morally wrong, but because "nobody tells me what to do!")—and that is boomeritis. It was a culture of narcissism, but a narcissism hiding out in very highly developed ideals. It wasn't just red; it was green infected with red.

Already green's pathological dimensions were starting to dysfunctionally infect anything in its path, and we saw what that narcissistic underbelly has done to culture ever since green became the leading-edge. A broken green leading-edge pathologically activated narcissism and egocentrism all over the place. Education in particular was hit hard by this undercurrent of narcissism, and it hasn't really functioned well ever since. And it's not just its extreme versions—such as getting rid of grades altogether and giving everybody a gold star; or sporting events without any winners or losers, but rather where every single athlete who simply showed up was given the same medal; or instances of kids who literally cannot read getting accepted at colleges (who's to judge them?)—but that it's pandemically affected education at all levels. The whole "self-esteem" education movement is a classic example: don't teach the capacity to know truth anymore (since there is no truth), but rather teach how extraordinarily special I am— "the wonder of being me"—which actually resulted, as we saw, in a graduating class that expressed greater degrees of narcissism than any class since testing was begun.

Green's belief that, because no values are really real, all values are equally true (because equally false)—it's that pathological aperspectival madness that simply must be healed, and a discriminating wisdom reintroduced. It's not going to help to institute a universally free education for everybody if all we're producing are self-promoting narcissists by the droves. That in fact is a prescription for a true social disaster, accelerated by making sure that we include ever more people in the narcissism-producing machinery.

Given that green is the present (ersatz) leading-edge, comprising some 25 percent of the population, its fairly large numbers make it at least a possible candidate for making this change itself, given that it is now widely self-conscious that something is very, very wrong with what it has been doing (and Trump's election has cemented this suspicion: for every green that simply blames and hates Trump, another green has started to ask what it has itself done to help bring this about). The realization is slowly dawning that elite urban green, not just ethnocentric rural amber, drove Trump into office (a dynamic virtually nobody saw—hence the shock everywhere at Trump's election—and a dynamic that green has a profoundly difficult time understanding, or rather, admitting—we'll return to this point in just a minute).

One of the immediate effects of the self-correcting move of evolution itself has been that, after just a few weeks of Trump's being in office, the actual practical realities of a belief in "no truth" have started to become shockingly obvious to almost everybody, and around the world. Everything from "fake news" to "alternative facts" have made virtually every green in the world (along with everybody else) alarmingly aware of just how idiotic the "no truth" notion actually is—especially when its own truths are regularly and loudly being charged as "fake news." Teaching that "no truth" idea in an ivory tower, divorced from any practical reality, to unsuspecting college students is one thing; seeing it in real action is quite another. And around the world, coming out of essentially every university in existence, there has arisen a thunderous silence. Nobody, but nobody, will say that "there is no truth, only social fabrications." The "no truth" idea itself is not said, not spoken, not written, not posted, not published, not even whispered—except to argue that it's a totally mistaken notion. It's as if the past four decades of intense postmodern philosophizing have been thrown out the window: Derrida, Foucault, Lyotard, Lacan—all of them, gone! At least when it comes to that specific tenet. After hearing somebody like Trump constantly claiming that there is no truth and that all news agencies who disagree with him are fake news, no self-respecting scholar can even repeat those words. The notion itself has become a massive embarrassment. Instead—and no matter how much the majority of the rest of their beliefs still rest on the lynchpin of "no truth"—commentators from every direction have been going out of their way to maintain that "truth is what journalism is all about, it's what we strive to report, it's why we're here!" Unanimously they are condemning the notion that there is no truth and are ridiculing the idea that there could even be "alternative facts." The *New York Times* took out a million-dollar television ad that proudly concluded, "Truth is now more important than ever!" This central "no truth" aspect of the brokenness of green has been colossally ditched within a matter of weeks. It's absolutely hysterical.

This notion itself—that there is "no truth"—is the theoretical foundation on which all the other cherished green extremisms rely, including extreme egalitarianism, political correctness, absolutistic social equality, denial of free speech, and so on. The fact that it is definitely *not true* that there is no truth—astonishingly enough, that fact has indeed become fairly obvious, especially when its blatantly immediate ridiculousness has been made apparent by almost every word out of Trump's mouth. What absolutely no philosopher, no matter how great, has been able to do over the past four decades—not Habermas, not Taylor, none of them—Donald Trump managed to do within a month. Lord, when evolution self-corrects, it really self-corrects!

But the rest of those green extremisms will almost certainly take longer to cure—if they ever are. What we're discussing now is how to pursue this healing path forward, beyond merely recognizing the now-obvious silliness of "no truth" and going yet further to see the similar silliness of its many related extreme beliefs, and thus to help green return to a real leading-edge role in evolution. This will be measured precisely by the degree of the disappearance of the long list of mean-green-meme extremisms held by the lynchpin of "no truth" over the years (including extreme political correctness, exterior-only egalitarianism, absolutistic social equality, denial of free speech, oppression of comedy on campus, blindly forced safe spaces, trigger warnings, and so on). I do think this process will indeed be much slower than has happened for "no truth," but there are indications that it is at least moving forward.

Here's just one example of this—an example of a slowly but widely growing realization of green's complicity in the election of an amber ethnocentric Trump—and another indication that the self-correcting drive of evolution is indeed kicking in. In an online article by African American Jeremy Flood (cofounder of At the Margins), entitled "The Revolution Must Be Felt," after emphasizing that Trump's election was the victory of a strong ethnocentric current, Flood very perceptively confesses, "But in the very same vein, we [liberals] must acknowledge the way in which we refer to Trump's base, the way we emphasize his support from the 'non-college educated,' the way we approach the premise of rural white America generally, relies on that very same prejudicial inference. **Our hatred for these people is at its very essence classism** [his bold; it is, in other words, an ethnocentric hatred of ethnocentrism]. This cannot be stressed enough. Contempt for white ruralites is built into the fabric of the modern liberal lexicon. We set them up as a vessel of every oppressive construct university liberalism has aimed to dismantle [i.e., as we saw earlier, the single great cause of all forms of oppression]—from fundamentalist religion, to sine qua non nationalism, to a general distrust in science, we've sculpted these people into a caricature of barbarian ignorance. And then, when we come knocking for votes, we expect them not to have noticed. In taking these peoples' votes for granted while unabashedly airing our hostility, we pushed them ever closer to the precipice, and then watched in shock as they jumped." Angry indeed.

Flood continues, "And if our own classism prevents us from

caring about the emotional needs of those we deride as deplorable, we are not really progressives." He explains:

> Do you disagree with the substance of this narrative? Are you aching to insert how [their] views are misleading, the byproduct of sexism, unfair media attention, and double standards? Me too. It doesn't matter. That was the narrative that we sold to millions of people. And they told us what they thought of it. We lost Michigan. We lost Pennsylvania. We lost Ohio. The razed waste of Unionland. How did we get here?

How indeed? Says Flood, "Pundits can argue forever about whether economic or racial anxiety triggered the detonation. But here is the bottom line: **the Left failed** [his bold]. We failed not because we didn't have the facts on our side, not because our policies weren't better for the working class, not because the redneck sods of the Trumpian horde were too racist to see reason. The left failed because the story they were selling wasn't strong enough to overcome these *not at all new* resentments [his italics]."

Ressentiment, most definitely. Flood notes that "Solidarity is a story. It's composed of our actions and our authenticity. It's about collective [worldcentric] identity and collective struggle. We are not 'stronger together' when half of us are 'deplorable.'" Amen, brother. Our constant point: we simply cannot move forward as a nation when half of the people hate the other half. "We embraced an academic, impersonal style of politics [postmodern poststructuralist], and through our tone and narrative, the Democratic party came to embody exactly the kind of elitist hierarchy it was built to overcome."

Right on the money. Green was meant to overcome a dominator hierarchy, not a growth hierarchy. A growth hierarchy is actually how we overcome a dominator hierarchy in the first place. As we've seen, one of the primary reasons that this "failure of the Left" has come about is that whenever we deny growth hierarchies, then automatically, unavoidably, and by default, we strengthen dominator hierarchies. You don't have to do anything else at all, because we are all born with a native inclination to dominator hierarchies. Without a countervailing current that tilts, trends, and develops us toward our highest worldcentric and integral possibilities, we slide into our lowest common denominators, our egocentric and ethnocentric power drives. (And when originally worldcentric notions regress to ethnocentric displays, they take on the flavor of all amber-stage productions: an absolutistic, fundamentalist, "one-true-way" attitude, and we buy into it with a religious fervor that takes no prisoners. We have seen this happen with science itself, as it slid into amber scientific materialism and reductionistic scientism; with feminism, where for many, it slid into an absolutistic religion, the slightest disagreement with which was viewed as deeply, demonically sexist; we saw it with Marxism, as it slid into a de facto zealot religion for millions—while religion may or may not be the opiate of the masses, Marxism became the opiate of the intellectuals—and we've seen it with many political ideologies: even those coming from orange or green, when latched on to with an unquestioning fervor and absolutistic enthusiasm, slid into their lowest ethnocentric and even egocentric displays, with disaster a short step away.) When that happens, then this slide from growth holarchies into dominator hierarchies is deeply unavoidable—and catastrophic when it comes from the leading-edge itself. No wonder evolution imploded.

While several previously dysfunctional greens, such as the good Mr. Flood himself, are starting to realize the hand they played in the vast tide of resentment that landed Trump in office, few of them, as yet, fully grasp the need for growth holarchies to actually reverse the trend. The denial of hierarchy in general is an inherent tendency of the pluralistic/relativistic wave—it simply recoils in horror at the very thought that some stances could be "higher" or "better" or "more valuable" than others. (As we've seen, green deals with any and all hierarchies by using its own fake news.) *Any* such "judging" and "ranking" is viewed as the very core of all oppression and injustice and wicked power drives. Graves felt that, because green is the highest of the 1st-tier stages—and because nested hierarchies or holarchies are widely reintroduced as an intrinsic feature of all 2nd-tier integral stages—then green has an inbuilt hyper-sensitivity to all hierarchies, so it will approach the newly introduced 2nd-tier hierarchies with appropriate care and caution as it arrives at integral. Since dominator hierarchies truly are the source of much, if not all, social oppression and injustice, green needs to learn to be on guard for any judging, ranking, or valuing tendencies, and is motivated to undo them wherever they are found.

But that view in its unthinking and extreme form is just an overblown, reflex, knee-jerk reaction on green's part—and green doesn't really believe it all by itself, as we have often seen. The only way green can arrive at the thought that, for example, value judgments are bad, is to make a whole series of value judgments about it. Likewise, green has a ranking system that ranks no-ranking as better and more valuable than ranking—and that is itself most certainly a ranking. It has a very strong hierarchy, or value judgment, that puts hierarchies on its bottom levels and puts "no hierarchy" on its top levels—itself a hierarchy. It believes, as I have previously summarized it, that its view is definitely superior in a world where nothing is supposed to be superior. That's not "no judgment," that's a very definite and fervently embraced judgment! I'm repeating myself here, but the points are simply that (1) green's goals are quite highly developed, (2) but it has no way to officially legitimate or give believable reasons for its own goals, and (3) even worse, it has no path to its goals at all. Add them up, and you have a colossal failure of leading-edge direction.

So what green needs to learn to do, after it gets over its initial and not-well-thought-out reaction against all hierarchies and all value judgments entirely, is to realize that it is only able to reach its conclusions in the first place because it has its own version of value judgments and hierarchical attitudes—these are impossible to avoid. Thus, instead of pretending to get rid of judgments and rankings and hierarchies altogether—which it can't really do anyway, which is why it keeps expressing its own versions of these—it needs to distinguish between what is a good, true, real, and ethical form of hierarchical judgment—which green tends to possess (compared to earlier stages)—versus what is a corrupt, dominating, oppressive, and unjust form of hierarchical judgment (which the lower stages tend to possess). And coming to the conclusion that, all things considered, worldcentric/integral values are indeed better than egocentric/ethnocentric values (as highest ideals), it will come straight to the distinction between actualization (or growth) hierarchies versus dominator (or oppressive) hierarchies. Growth holarchies have the profound advantage of themselves following directly a real genealogy, a real evolutionary current, a real developmental/historical process that unfolds in some 6-to-8 major stages of increasingly inclusive, increasingly loving, increasingly caring, increasingly whole and conscious and complex and inclusive—and increasingly less domineering, less oppressive, less unjust—forms, and which we summarize as the ever-expanding growth from egocentric to ethnocentric to worldcentric to integral (or selfish to care to universal care to integrated).

Using these growth holarchies, a healthy green can see immediately that these were in fact the actual basis of its original judgments and original rankings—that these growth hierarchies are what it actually had in mind when it condemned dominator hierarchies. It didn't mean to stop making all judgments entirely—green itself was making judgments left and right. It meant to stop making racist, sexist, misogynistic, homophobic, xenophobic, and similarly prejudiced judgments (that is, stop making ethnocentric judgments), and to start making judgments that are worldcentric, all-embracing, postconventional, and truly inclusive—those are the judgments we are most definitely supposed to make (at least as ideals)! And those judgments are based on the growth hierarchy through which we need to move—from ethnocentric (and lower) to worldcentric (and higher)—if we are to reach and express our own truest potentials. So stop making oppressive/ethnocentric judgments and rankings and hierarchies, and start making worldcentric/integral judgments and rankings and hierarchies. Ah, now it all fits!

Furthermore, in realizing this, green is likewise immediately released from its endless performative contradictions. To give merely one major example: it's released from its unending claims that it is universally true that there is no universal truth. Now what green really means is this: Because all truth has a historical dimension (which itself is a universal truth), and because in the past what was taken as "truth" was often a partial, prejudiced, and bigoted "truth" (which marginalized and oppressed various groups), then we want to be aware of this nasty possibility. And therefore we are going to point these nasty factors out, and when we do so, we mean that what we are saying applies to all cultures, at all times, in all places. And thus, what we are really saying is that here are some universal worldcentric truths that will help us combat and prevent ethnocentric and oppressive truths. Presented in that light, then all of green's rankings and value judgments on the horrors of ethnocentric truth can pour forth, in a fully *noncontradictory* and *truthful* fashion. And it is indeed expressing universal truths when it does so (truths that become available at the green level and express perspectives that are enacted and manifest at that level for the first time). Because green is coming from a very high level of growth hierarchy, it can condemn and criticize the dominator hierarchies that spring from lower levels.

That is the overall realization—growth holarchies are how we overcome dominator hierarchies—that is central to green's healing its fractured, broken, absolutistic, ersatz-elitist, and de facto oppressive slide into its own disastrous and self-contradictory forms of ethnocentric and fundamentalist ideology. And thus it will be able to return to its genuine functional role as a truly *leading* leading-edge, marshalling a collective humanity's self-organization through self-transcendence.

So this process of a broken green fundamentally healing its own level and returning to its central and much more healthy "true but partial" tenets is one possibility for a way forward. This depends, *first*, on green's releasing its perverse hostility to virtually every previous stage of development that came before it. Not deplorable, but compassionately empathized. And *second*—and more difficult—is to realize that the actual basis of green's "negative" judgment about the previous stages is the fact that all previous stages are indeed less inclusive, less embracing, less complex, and less conscious than is green in its healthy forms (because they are all lower levels of growth and inclusiveness). And that is most certainly true, and is grounded in an authentic genealogy, a true evolutionary/historical unfolding. But the healthy, correct, just reaction to such realities is an attitude of outreach, of embrace, of compassion and care. Each higher stage—green in this case—inherently "transcends and includes" its predecessors. But despising them, loathing them, actually hating them is to "transcend and repress," "transcend and exclude," "transcend and ridicule"—at which point one's right and one's capacity to be a genuine leading-edge is forfeited, which green most certainly has done.

Working against the possibility of a green self-healing is the fact that green itself, in whatever form, is an actual stage of development; it's a worldview, and in that sense, it operates like a paradigm (as Kuhn originally meant the term). And the thing about paradigms is that, whether functional or dysfunctional, they are notoriously hard to get rid of. Max Planck (creator of the notion of a "quantum" of energy, thus ushering in the quantum mechanics revolution) is credited with being the first to notice that, paraphrased, "Old paradigms die when the believers in old paradigms die"—which I summarized as "The knowledge quest proceeds funeral by funeral." The point is that, put bluntly, boomeritis might die only when the Boomers die. But seeing the millennials adopting many of these notions, sometimes in even more extreme forms, it doesn't look like death is anywhere near strong enough to get rid of a really bad thing.

For green to move forward and begin actions that would lead to its genuine self-healing, the two steps that I summarized above (drop its reactive hatred and hostility to all previous value levels, and do so by adopting growth holarchies that inherently combat dominator hierarchies) are both mandatory, in my opinion. My sense is that the first step will be much easier and that, indeed, the first step has already begun in many cases. But the second step is a huge one for green, and we will probably have to simply move on to the next major possibility for humanity's moving forward, if this second step is to be widely implemented.

I'll come back to my thoughts on exactly which way that is most likely to go. But first let's go ahead and explore that other major possibility of an effective response to a Trump presidency (and why such a response is actually possible and now available).

10 : Another Way Forward: Truly Integral

The other possibility that would work to help the present self-correcting dynamic of evolution to actually get some traction would be to introduce not a healthy green (although that would always help), but to directly introduce a turquoise integral-stage leading-edge (or 2nd tier in general). This will happen, come what may, at some future point. (We know this to be so because every single developmental model now in existence, with virtually no exceptions, has found in its own research that, beyond any pluralistic or relativistic stages, there are one or more integral or systemic stages, and these stages integrate the fragmented differentiations created by green. What that means is that, even though the percentage of people at integral stages is now only around 5 percent, those stages have already become a repeating habit, and thus have already been laid down, for the most part, as Kosmic grooves or currents that are available to all humans who continue their growth and development.)

And there is no reason some aspects of an integral stage cannot start to take hold now. The reason this would be so effective is that, while green can push itself and strive to be more open, understanding, and compassionate toward all previous levels (which now exist as stations of life in society), the integral stage does this automatically, inherently, and in a much deeper, more authentic fashion. We saw that the integral stage is the first developmental stage in all of history that feels that every previous stage has a great deal of importance and significance. It does not necessarily agree with them, but it fully accepts and embraces them (though not their limitations)—if nothing else, each previous stage is indeed a stage in an overall human development, and no stage can be skipped or bypassed. Loathing previous stages is deeply, deeply suicidal. The integral stage thinks that each previous stage is important, while each previous stage itself thinks that only *it* is important. Hence the leap to integral truly being "cataclysmic," "monumental."

That is why an Integral approach (capitalized when it means a specific theory and practice) would almost automatically end the disasters of an aperspectival madness, and restore the leading-edge's capacity to actually lead. This, after all, is exactly what the self-correcting move of evolution itself is attempting to introduce. And anybody adopting an Integral stance is riding the very leading-edge of evolution itself, with all of its goodness, truth, and beauty. This is yet another—although "monumentally" new, different, and greater—degree of "order out of chaos."

The other major advantage of an integral leading-edge is that it would create an enormously powerful downward-acting morphic field that would exert a strong pressure on green to heal its fragmented and broken ways. Although this would not in itself directly cure each and every green defect—that can be done only with green's own actions and cooperation—it would nonetheless introduce a powerful regenerative field that would compensate for green's malfunctions and in many cases would indeed help green to directly heal them. In general, then, this second way forward would tend to include within it much of the first way forward, transcending and including it in an altogether more embracing fashion (with an ideal way forward including a good deal of both).

This is just one of the things that an integral leading-edge would accomplish. But the stunningly far-reaching effects of a truly integral leading-edge is something that we of today can barely fathom—and for the simple reason that humanity has never, at any point, had anything like this in its entire history. Never have we had a leading-edge that truly embraced and included every previous stage. We have no precedents for this whatsoever; we have no idea what this might be like. It is so dramatically different from any previous situation that it almost falls into the category of science fiction. But we did see that when around 10 percent of the population reaches the same level as that of the leading-edge itself, then there is something of a "tipping point" reached, and the generic qualities of the leading-edge tend to seep into or permeate the entire culture. We already have around 5 percent that is already at integral, and it might reach 10 percent within a decade or two. At that time, there would be a transformative shift in the interior domains the likes of which humanity has never, but never, seen. The true *inclusiveness* that forward-thinking social and political theorists have long idolized as near utopian would in fact become a very real possibility for humanity for the first time in its entire history.

This will be happening at about the same time that we reach something resembling a technological Singularity—and together, these conditions would propel the world into a transformative event the likes of which has never been remotely seen—or even imagined—before. This will be in direct opposition to many of the present-day degenerative, degrading, divisive, devolving currents that are the product of an abundance of lower stages—that, among other items, drive terrorism, intense marginalization, global warming, environmental degradation, and social injustices such as trafficking—and that are also now actually headed by a leading-edge that has disastrously derailed. These are truly dangerous times. That is why the beginning of a genuinely Integral Age—in all 4 quadrants—will arrive not a moment too soon. I could go on endlessly here, but I'll simply leave that tantalizing possibility to your imagination. I will point out that this integral stage, because it has already started to emerge in full force around the world, has, among a huge number of other things, created entire theories that originate at this newly emergent level—with

Integral Metatheory, which I represent, being one of the most effective, having already fully reinterpreted over 60 human disciplines through an Integral lens—giving items such as Integral Business, Integral Medicine, Integral Art, Integral History, Integral Spirituality, Integral Economics, Integral Education, Integral Politics, and so on—each one of them a much more effective and inclusive approach to its field.

But one of our central points, for either major way forward, is essentially the same, which I'll briefly summarize: the green postmodern leading-edge of evolution itself has, for several decades, degenerated into its extreme, pathological, and dysfunctional forms. As such, it is literally incapable of effectively acting as a real leading-edge. Its fundamental belief—"there is no truth" (with its many derivatives)—and its basic essential attitude—"aperspectival madness"—cannot in any fashion actually lead, actually choose a course of action that is positive, healthy, effective, and truly evolutionary. With all growth hierarchies denied and deconstructed, evolution has no real way to grow, has no way forward at all, and thus nothing but dominator hierarchies are seen everywhere, effectively reducing any individual you want to a victim. The leading-edge has collapsed; it is now a few-billion-person massive car crash, a huge traffic jam at the very edge of evolution itself, sabotaging virtually every move that evolution seeks to take. Evolution itself finds its own headlights shining beams of nihilism, which can actually see nothing, or beams of narcissism, which can see only itself. Under this often malicious leadership ("the mean green meme"), the earlier levels and stages of development have themselves begun to hemorrhage, sliding into their own forms of pathological dysfunction. And this isn't just happening in one or two countries, it is happening around the world.

This culturally divisive and fragmenting force (in the Lower Left) has joined with various systemic forces (in the Lower Right), such as a technological drive toward divisive, echo-chambered, and siloed individuals, and an interior drive (in the Upper Left) toward increasingly narcissistic displays. With no overriding drives to cohesion, unity, or self-organization available in a truly effective fashion in any of the quadrants, there is an almost historically unprecedented regression in essentially all of them. Evolution, in a decided move of self-correction, has paused and is in the process of backing up a few paces, regrouping, and reconstituting itself for a healthier, more unified, more functional continuation. What virtually all of these regroupings have as a primary driver is a profound anti-green dynamic acting as a morphic field radiating from the broken leading-edge itself.

Donald Trump, more than any other single factor, has (unknown to himself, or virtually anybody else, for that matter) ridden these anti-green forces to a massively surprising presidential victory. As previous stages became, in various ways and to various degrees, activated by Trump, whether orange, amber, or red, they all shared one thing: the anti-green dynamic (a dynamic that, because it had not been recognized in any significant way, made Trump's victory a stunning and unbelievable surprise to virtually everybody). And—although Trump himself will do little to actually address the details of this—as each of these stages works to redress the imbalances inflicted on it by an extreme green and its aperspectival madness, the overall effects of these recent events could indeed turn out to be quite healthy, allowing evolution to generally self-correct and adopt a leading-edge that can actually lead, thus allowing evolution itself to continue its ongoing march of "transcend and include," a self-organization through self-transcendence.

THE LIKELY FUTURE

In order for that to happen, not only do the various earlier stages (red, amber, and orange) need to throw off the deconstructed shambles inflicted on each by an unhealthy green, but green itself has to heal, has to become truly functional again, has to reject its nihilism and narcissism, has to let go of its aperspectival madness, has to learn the difference between dominator hierarchies and growth holarchies and introduce a developmental-based discriminating wisdom, in order for evolution to again start moving forward in a truly self-organizing and self-transcending way.

The one other option, slightly different, is for evolution to leapfrog to an integral stage of unfolding as its new leading-edge, which would inherently perform all the tasks now required of a regenerated green. This "leapfrogging" would not constitute skipping a stage (which is not possible), but it would mean building a higher stage on a diseased predecessor, which lands it with a handicap right from the start. The integral attitude, however, is designed to effectively spot and route around such roadblocks, and this we would expect to see.

The most likely course of action, however, is some mixture of both. That's not a cop-out, it's a precise prediction. Green simply cannot function, not even on its own level, if it continues in the extreme, mean-green-meme (vindictively seeing "deplorables" everywhere), hyper-sensitive, over-the-top politically correct, dysfunctional, and pathological form in which it now exists. Its inherent contradictions are increasingly being seen and felt, and ways to work around them are being explored (which incorporate the partial truths of green but not their extreme and pathological absolutisms). We've already seen that one of the immediate effects of Trump's election is that, even in the universities themselves, almost nobody will even utter "there is no truth," not in an approving fashion, anyway, but often to actually ridicule its deep idiocy. This is already a profound self-correction.

(I've been dealing with rampant "no-truth" theorists for four decades; I honestly cannot now imagine a single respected scholar anywhere claiming or writing that "there is no truth." What we are going to see, in the next decade or two, is a furious backpedaling and hair-splitting about "no truth"—trying to explain what was "really meant" by "no truth," things like, "Various historical currents can set up situations where certain truths have real legitimate value for a given length of time," etc.—but the central notion itself will have nothing of the gravity that it had for nearly half a century, nor will it have the completely uncontested ability to simply deconstruct any and all other "truths," virtually all of which were disdainfully dismissed with the single gambit of pulling the rug of truth out from under them. That, truly, is dead. And so to postmodernism's endless proclamations of the "end of" and the "death of"—the end of humanism, the end of the subject, the end of individuality, the end of consciousness, the end of representation, the end of the Enlightenment, the end of patriarchy, the end of objectivism, the end of rationality, the end of modernism, the end of man—we can now add: the end of postmodernism's no truth. And the embarrassing footnote very well might read: "thanks to Donald J. Trump." It seems to have taken an actual buffoon-in-action, displaying the utter absurdity of such a notion day in and day out, to make an inherently obvious idiocy finally obvious in a way that could no longer be denied with any sort of integrity. Especially noteworthy is that virtually all mainstream media—which had spent the better part of the last four decades spewing out their belief in essentially every other major tenet of liberal postmodern egalitarianism—fell all over themselves jumping to the defense of truth and screaming its central importance for their very existence, starting with no less than the *Times*: "Truth is now more important than ever!" That sentiment is utterly inconceivable coming out of postmodern academia anytime during the past half century—until just about three weeks after Trump's inauguration, and now it is the banner headline under which all good men and women everywhere are meant to march. Honestly, in my entire professional career, I have never seen anything this . . . weird, odd, yet fully welcomed.)

Further, a significant number of green individuals, instead of simply bemoaning and reviling Trump and his many supporters, have begun instead to realize that they themselves must begin doing the one thing they previously despised: they have to try to reach out, to understand, to include in the dialogue, and to extend the courtesy of a rudimentary amount of compassion, care, even love, to the whole basket of deplorables—which embodies an understanding on green's part that green itself might indeed have directly contributed to the anger, resentment, sometimes hatred, that the core of Trump's supporters expressed and that directly drove Trump into office. Yes, many of Trump's voters were clearly and deeply amber ethnocentric. But all too often it was green's reviling, ridiculing, despising, and vengeful attitude that directly contributed to turning typical amber into a seething, deeply resentful, angry, and even hateful cauldron of truly vicious amber. (And remember, a staggering 81 percent of that angry crowd voted Trump.) Thus, as we noted, it is broken green, not just amber, that drove Trump into office (a dynamic, again, that virtually nobody saw, hence the universal shock at the election results—and the deep, deep difficulty that green has in understanding its own complicity in Trump's election).

But now that "anti-green" message is starting to get across to many greens themselves, and hence the anti-green morphic field is having its intended effect—which is the overall drive toward a softening and more inclusive embrace, across the spectrum, of each stage of development, an embrace that should be evidenced to some degree by each of the stages themselves, but an embrace lived in an exemplary fashion by the leading-edge itself—*if* it is to really lead.

In the present situation, where essentially 50 percent of the country hates the other 50 percent, those two major groups are fundamentally anchored in the amber and the green, and the problem is, the hatred is perfectly mutual. Green hates the amber deplorables, and amber certainly hates the green elites right back. So the argument always develops around which group first should stop the hating and start the loving? And it's always a heated argument: "Why should I go first?" But the answer here, in reality, is quite simple: Who's more evolved?

The lessening of green's pervasive hostility and vindictiveness toward all previous stages of development is what we identified as "step one" in the requisite self-healing of green. There is at least a decent likelihood that this will begin—and to some degree already has begun. On the other hand, "step two"—the realization that growth holarchies provide the actual basis of the value judgments that green is already making, and that these growth holarchies also are the only truly effective means to displace the dominator hierarchies that green correctly *ranks* on the bottom of the list of social desirables—is a bit less likely to occur at the green level itself, but will most likely depend upon the transformation to integral 2nd tier.

My strong suspicion, therefore, is that green will perform a good deal of step one on its own, and that this will have a very positive effect on the culture at large. And conversely, to the extent that at least this first step is not taken, then the self-corrective drive of evolution will continue to push, and push, and push into existing affairs, driving more Trump-like "disasters" as evolution redoubles its efforts to force its way through these recalcitrant obstructions.

But step two will likely be taken at this time only by integral communities themselves, and otherwise will await the growth of 10 percent of the population to integral, which would initiate a tipping point and propel the integral stage into being the next-higher leading-edge, with altogether stunning repercussions.

Contributing to this growth and increase in truly inclusive awareness, and under the drive to discover "what's next" after postmodernism, various Integral theories and metatheories are increasingly gaining ground, and wherever they do, they automatically correct the green dysfunctions that they unearth. Little by little, in other words, an Integral awareness is helping to embody an evolutionary self-correction in its very actions.

One of the central items in an Integral approach is the inclusion of the reality of the developmental aspects of human beings. That's only one component of Integral Metatheory, but it's an important component that, as I have often stated, is almost always overlooked or ignored—with disastrous consequences. Disastrous, because these developmental pathways are the actual routes to truly achieving real diversity and inclusion. It's time to approach worldcentric diversity and integral inclusion with more than passionately embraced slogans. Simply approaching every person we see out of 100 as if they already are predisposed, capable, and eager to embrace those worldcentric values is to deeply undercut the real path to those values. Look to interiors, not just exteriors. Robert Kegan, the Harvard developmentalist that I have already mentioned, works with many organizations, business and otherwise, helping them to facilitate their team members' development through exactly the types of growth stages that we have been talking about, moving them, as appropriate, from egocentric to ethnocentric to worldcentric to integral stances. (It's not beside the point to mention that these businesses almost always show substantial leaps in productivity.) Kegan calls these "deliberately developmental organizations," or DDOs. The point here is that these individuals actually engage, and proceed through, real developmental unfoldings on the way to their truly higher, wider, more inclusive capacities—not just slogans or claims or passionate beliefs, but genuine growth and developmental realities. Not just changes in their exteriors, but real and lasting changes in their interiors.

And if we are going to come anywhere close to ending the disasters of a merely 1st-tier culture—a society defined by its culture wars of amber against orange against green, a society of ethnocentric enthusiasms claiming ultimate value, a culture wracked by indecision anchored in post-truth confusion, a society where fully half of its members hate the other half—then we are going to have to move from a culture of no-truth to a DDC: *a deliberately developmental culture.*

That is just one of the core conclusions of the Integral view. But it is the component that we have focused on the most in this book—namely, the importance of growth holarchies for overcoming dominator hierarchies and curing a culture of post-truth. It is the overall Integral view that I wish to recommend to any who are ready for such. It deliberately and self-consciously embraces every perspective that it encounters (literally), and thus not only provides the balm for a world gone slightly mad with fragmented, siloed, broken shards and slivers of reality, but can bring together not just various people but various approaches to truth itself, resulting in truly comprehensive and integral overviews of the Good, the True, and the Beautiful. It is grounded in the newly emergent, most inclusive, most unified, and most embracing stages of development and evolution yet to emerge (which "transcend and include" every single previous stage, thus ensuring real comprehensiveness)—and is not merely based on an idea (as is, say, pragmatism), but is grounded in the actual territory of a level of development of being and awareness itself (namely, the integral stage/s).

This provides a means for us to Show Up (in all of our dimensions or quadrants of being); Grow Up (through all our levels of development and lines of development); Wake Up (to all of our states of consciousness, including those called Enlightenment, Awakening, Metamorphosis, Moksha, Satori, the Great Liberation); and Clean Up (our shadow elements driving epidemic emotional dys-eases). In embracing all of yesterday, it opens us to all of tomorrow. And it will provide a leading-edge of evolution the likes of which humanity has literally never seen before.

This is indeed the next, authentic and genuine leading-edge, and it has already begun its inevitable emergence. It carries with it the inexorable drive to "transcend and include" literally all of the previous stages of development and the stations of life that they now inhabit—but minus the inherent rancor that each of them, on its own, feels for the others. It is indeed "cataclysmic," "a monumental leap in meaning," and it is here for each of us to embrace and express right now, should we so desire. And it is the one, sure, and certain balm—if authentically inhabited—for the isolating, regressive, repressive, mean-spirited, and fragmenting state in which the world now finds itself rapidly drowning.

Seeing this bigger picture, this Integral overview, allows us to escape the suffocating suffering of focusing solely on a Trump win. Conversely, feeling nothing but despair at Trump's victory is to fail to see the larger currents at work in this situation. Understanding this election—as well as similar events now occurring all over the world—as a manifestation of a self-correcting drive of evolution itself, as it routes around a broken leading-edge green and attempts to restore the capacity of its leading-edge to actually lead (while also seriously starting to give birth to the next-higher leading-edge of integral itself)—this gives us a glimmer of real hope in an otherwise desperately gloomy situation.

In the deepest parts of our own being, each of us is directly one with this evolutionary current, this Eros, this Spirit-in-action, radiant to infinity and luminous to eternity, radically full in its overflowing superabundance and excessive in its good graces, wildly crashing off the heavens and irreverently irrupting from the underworlds, unconditionally embracing each and all in its limitless love and care. And the only ones who should be allowed to work politically for a greater tomorrow—and who should indeed thus work—are those who truly understand that it is not necessary to do so, who see the utter fullness of the Great Perfection in each and every moment of existence, and who nonetheless work to trim-tab (or adjust through leadership) the manifestation of more and more and more of the Good and the True and the Beautiful—right here and right now in this gloriously manifest universe, moment to moment to ever-present moment—knowing full well that this entire world is nothing but the dream of an infinite Spirit, yet each and every one of us directly being, in reality, this very Spirit itself, dreaming the world of our own amazement.

And we can try endlessly and tirelessly to fix this dream . . . or we can simply wake up.

Or—the true and ultimate secret—we can discover the integral embrace that actually does both, thus totally freeing us (by ending the dream) and completely fulfilling us (by fixing it), miraculously performed fully and together in one and the same instant, now to now to endlessly now . . .

Afterword to the 2024 Edition: An Overview of the Integral Model

We live in difficult times. And we seem to have few choices about what to do about it. All in all, it's just a dull, drab, fragmented, and polarized world out there. The only real choices that we have lie within, in our capacity to form and mold our own philosophy and worldview. And yet, we are culturally given very few options in that area, either. Many people don't even have a developed philosophy or a vigorous worldview; they just sort of sleep along from day to day, playing it by ear as they bumble forward.

You might have opened this book with an interest in politics, but it also offers you a real alternative, a way to create a genuine, philosophically sophisticated, integrated worldview, one that is very easy to learn and even simpler to apply. And what's more, it shows you how to pull your world together, because it's very complete and inclusive. In fact, it claims to integrate virtually all of the known disciplines of knowledge—science, religion, art, history, sociology, business, psychology—in one nifty and self-contained framework.

As you're probably starting to see, Integral Theory integrates and unites all of the various different and often apparently conflicting approaches of our knowledge into unified and easily grasped areas, to give us Integral Psychology, Integral Business, Integral Spirituality, Integral Art, Integral Sociology, Integral Philosophy, and on and on, all wonderfully fitted together in the very same Integral Framework. For those interested in taking this further, I offer a brief recap of some elements of the theory we've already discussed, along with a deeper explanation and overview of some key areas.

The Integral Framework is often known in short as "AQAL"—which stands for "all quadrants, all levels, all lines, all states, and all types"—which are the five major elements of the Framework itself. The "quadrants" (of which there are three or four major ones, including 1st-person, 2nd-person, and 3rd-person pronouns) stand for the basic, fundamental perspectives that all human beings have, and through which they view the world around them. These quadrants are so fundamental and widespread that entire classes of pronouns are named after them—as already mentioned, "1st-person," "2nd-person," and "3rd-person" pronouns being the most common. 1st person represents the perspective of "the person speaking" (or the 1st-person viewpoint, such as I, me, or mine); 2nd person is the perspective or the view of "the person being spoken to" (or 2nd-person viewpoint, such as you, thou, or yours); and 3rd person is the perspective of "the person or thing being spoken about" (or 3rd-person viewpoint, such as he, her, they, them, it, or its).

Each of those classes of pronouns is further divided into inside versus outside, or subject versus object (subjective I or mine versus objective they or it), and also singular versus plural (singular me versus plural them), which, when combined, gives us the inside and the outside of the singular and the plural, which are the 4 quadrants, or the four basic perspectives that we all have access to. Notice that these are all very real realities; they all exist; and each one gives us a different viewpoint of the world. The way they are all first laid out in Integral Theory—namely, as four boxes in a four-square figure—puts the insides on the Left-Hand quadrants, the outsides on the Right-Hand, and the singular in the Upper quadrants and the plural (or collective) in the Lower, overall giving us the Upper-Left quadrant (or 1st-person singular:

I, me, mine), the Lower-Left quadrant (or 1st-person plural, we or us, which contain a 1st-person I and a 2nd-person you). Then there are the outside or objective or 3rd-person views, the Upper-Right 3rd-person singular (he, she, it), and the Lower-Right 3rd-person collective or plural (they, them, its).

Each of these quadrant-perspectives are so real they even have different epistemologies and ontologies. The Upper-Left singular quadrant (I, me, mine) has *introspection*, or knowledge gained by looking within. The Lower-Left plural quadrant (we, us, ours) has *hermeneutics*, or the knowledge gained by interpretation (I understand you by interpreting what you say and do). The outside Upper-Right singular quadrant (he, she, it) has *empiricism*, or individual objective knowledge gained by the senses (which is a viewpoint often adopted by science, which likes to focus on individual things—an atom, a molecule, a tree, a fish—that can be seen objectively with the senses—hence, "empirical science" as it's often called). And the outside Lower-Right collective quadrant has *systems theory*, or the knowledge gained about objective whole systems (which is also a view often adopted by science, principally because the Right-Hand quadrants are all outside objective viewpoints, which allows science to be empirical and objective, hence its adoption of both Upper-Right and Lower-Right quadrants as its specialties).

As demonstrated throughout what you've read, these epistemologies (and their correlative ontologies), in one form or another, cover virtually all of the known areas of human knowledge. It's important to note that each of those quadrants is composed of "holons." As explained earlier, a holon is a whole that is simultaneously a part of another whole. A whole letter is part of a whole word, a whole word is part of a whole sentence, a whole sentence is part of a whole paragraph, a whole paragraph is part of a whole book, a whole magazine, a whole encyclopedia. Likewise, a whole proton is part of a whole nucleus, which is part of a whole cell, which is part of a whole organism (which is part of a whole species, which is part of the whole plant or animal kingdom). And so on. Every single, actually existing, objective individual thing (mental or physical) is actually a holon, as Koestler pointed out. Everything else is a heap, like a heap of garbage, no intrinsic shape or structure. But every actually existing whole is also a part of another whole, indefinitely (although the sequence does eventually wind out—atoms to molecules to cells to fish to amphibians to reptiles to mammals to humans to the earth and the solar system to the galaxy to the entire universe—the end).

All holons in all 4 quadrants undergo some form of development or evolution. The holons in the Upper-Left individual quadrant (1st-person I, me, mine) go through various *stages* or *levels* of evolution or development, which Jean Gebser identified as the "archaic stage," the "magic stage," the "mythic," the "rational," the "pluralistic," and the "integral" stages. Likewise, cultural holons in the plural Lower-Left quadrant go through a collective version of those same levels, each level of which is composed of many of the singular holons in the Upper-Left quadrant (they are, after all, their collective or plural forms). The various stages of these collective or plural levels of cultural holons are often named after the dominant individual holon that existed at that time or that stage or that level. For example, when the rational individual level became prominent during the modern era, it was often referred to as the "Age of Reason." But the point is that culture, like all the other quadrants, undergoes a development or evolution. In fact, the development in the Upper-Right, objective, individual quadrant is often simply referred to as "evolution" itself, since the whole string of holons in that individual, outside, objective Right-Hand quadrant was generally the first recognized series of holons to undergo an overall evolution in real life and time— protons and neutrons came together, and joined with electrons to form atoms; atoms joined together to develop molecules; molecules came together and formed living cells; cells came together to evolve into multicellular organisms; those organisms themselves evolved into increasingly higher forms, such as fish to amphibians to reptiles to mammals to humans, and the whole chain of life thus evolved. And at each of those individual stages of evolution, there were their corresponding collective, group, or plural forms. Atoms and molecules came together into whole crystals; large molecular crystals joined together into whole multimolecular living cells; living cells evolved into organisms that lived together in ecosystems; ecosystems formed entire forests; entire forests ended up existing on larger continents; continents formed whole planets; planets were part of an entire solar system; solar systems joined together into galaxies; the sum total of all galaxies and their stars is usually referred to as the "the universe." Whatever we call it, it is the product of a collective evolution of its individual holons, both singular and plural.

So there we have quadrants and their levels or stages of evolutionary unfolding. And notice that each *level* of evolution contains many various *lines* of evolution, or different kinds of holons that are evolving through the various levels that are available. The Upper-Left quadrant, for example, which consists of the insides of an individual 1ˢᵗ-person holon (I, me, mine), goes through cognitive development, emotional development, the development of various kinds of defense mechanisms, moral development, linguistic development, aesthetic development, and upward of a dozen different kinds or lines of "multiple intelligences." All of those *lines* of development grow and evolve through the very same basic *levels* of development—which gives us quadrants, levels, and lines.

A "level of development or evolution" is often called a "*structure*" of consciousness, because it is made of basic structures or patterns, much like language is made of grammar or syntactic structures. These are basic enduring structures, like patterns on a map, that are the same in all individual beings. They look the same, they emerge through the same major developmental stages, and they remain in existence once they have emerged, just as atoms and molecules stay in existence once they have emerged and formed into cells, and even as they become parts of these larger wholes, they retain their basic characteristics. Once an atom becomes part of a molecule, that atom remains fully and totally a real atom—it's just a real and whole atom that's now an actual part of a whole molecule (which is a part of a whole cell, which is part of a whole multicellular plant or animal, and so on). Those all fall under the general rubric of a basic structure. Much like building a brick house, with each whole brick—while remaining perfectly itself as a real brick—becoming incorporated into a larger whole structure, perhaps a particular room in the house, or a big wall, or a garage building, and so on—all the while retaining the same basic brick structure—that structure doesn't substantially change.

So those are enduring basic structures. As I said, when you possess a basic structure, you generally don't know that you have it. It's just like the rule or syntax structures of grammar. You are right now fully following a staggeringly large number of rules of grammar or syntax, but can you list them all, write them all down? No. They tend to be 3rd-person objective realities that just don't enter your 1st-person realities or knowledge (unless you formally study them). But you use them fully and accurately anyway, or you wouldn't be able to understand a thing that I am saying. But these "unconscious" structures are the building blocks of all of our lines of growth and levels of growth—they are the main ingredients of what I call Growing Up, Opening Up, and Showing Up—and play an important role in Cleaning Up.* Each of those areas is built or made up of enduring or *basic structures* of consciousness. (And, of course, all of them are holons.)

---

* For more about this topic, see my book *Finding Radical Wholeness: The Integral Path to Unity, Growth, and Delight* (Shambhala, 2024). Growing Up takes you through levels of development; Opening Up works further with the important lines in your life; Showing Up includes the important quadrants in your life; and Cleaning Up encompasses shadow work. Also important is Waking Up, which works with states of consciousness.

But there is another very major "building block" in our aware-ness that is extremely important, especially when it comes to the areas of Enlightenment or Awakening—which overall we refer to as the very important integral area generally called Waking Up—and these are known as *states* of consciousness. The main difference between structures and states is that *structures* operate mostly pre-consciously or flat-out unconsciously, whereas *states* operate fully consciously. So, in short, when you are using a real structure of consciousness—speaking a language, growing up though any number of multiple intelligences in the developmen-tal line of Growing Up, using any of the other dozens of multiple lines of development—moral, aesthetic, truthful, spatial, linguis-tic, among many others—all of those areas are built most pri-marily of the basic structures of consciousness, and so when you are using any of those, you will not be aware that you are using structures or the many rules that surround them. For example, when you grow from the stage or level known as "concrete opera-tional thinking" to the stage of "formal operational thinking" (in the overall cognitive line of Growing Up according to Jean Piag-et's work), all you will notice is that you are now speaking a type of reason and rationality; you won't also be aware of Aristotle's sixteen binary logical propositions that underlie rationality and are the sturdy building-block structures of consciousness that are the necessary supports for rational thinking. They very likely will not even cross your mind. Likewise, as you grow through the various stages of any of the Growing Up developmental levels in the various lines, you will barely remember the previous stage of development—you'll go from archaic to magic to mythic to rational to pluralistic to integral without even noticing much of those changes, because the basic structures are fast becoming pre-conscious.

Almost the exact opposite is true for states of consciousness. For one thing, states of consciousness are all fully 1st-person re-alities, not 3rd-person realities. In other words, they are all fully and totally in your experience and in your 1st-person awareness. That is, in fact, the very definition of 1st-person realities—direct experiences had by a living being. If, for example, you are out meditating in the woods, and all of a sudden you feel one with the entire universe in peace and love—believe me, you will know that experience fully and completely and consciously. None of it is hidden; it is fully your own 1st-person experience, which means by definition what you are fully and directly experiencing right now. Every *state* of consciousness is just like that—you experience all of it, fully, completely, and totally consciously. This state experience is vastly different from any *structure* experience, which you generally use without knowing it.

Thus, without actually studying the various types of experiences, stages, states, and structures, if a person has a really strong *state* experience of Enlightenment (or being One with the entire universe), they will nevertheless directly know they have had that Enlightenment experience of pure Oneness, and they will know what its major characteristics are. They will directly experience all of its features; none are hidden. They are one with the entire universe and they know it! But with *structures* of consciousness, when a person undergoes a real Growing Up development (which involves various lines—cognitive, emotional, aesthetic, moral, spiritual, and so forth—all moving through the same six levels or stages from archaic to magic to mythic to rational to pluralistic to integral)—when they move from any one of those levels to the next higher level—they will generally have no idea that they are at a totally new and different level or stage. All of us have gone through most of those six major levels of Growing Up, but virtually none of us remembers waking up one morning and going, "Hey, now I'm operating from a higher level or structure of consciousness!" In fact, we might have grown up through all six major levels of consciousness development (archaic to integral), but we don't remember six major times in our lives where we knew and recognized that we had moved up a significant level of development. When we move into the rational level, we don't realize that we are now speaking rationally, we simply start speaking rationally over a several-month period, and we have no idea that the structure of that level is an actual rational structure, just like we don't recognize the rules of grammar that underlie our common language structure (except sometimes if we are actually taught grammar in school, but we quickly forget those rules as they go pre-conscious). Neither you nor I can remember them now, nor do they come to mind as we use our language, although that language use does rely upon their pre-conscious existence.

This, by the way, fully accounts for the huge differences in the dates of discovery between disciplines relying on *states* of consciousness (such as Enlightenment practices of Waking Up) and those relying on *structures* of consciousness (such as Growing Up or Cleaning Up). Disciplines involving states of consciousness (like Enlightenment or Waking Up) were discovered at least 4,000 years earlier than the ones involving structures of consciousness (like Growing Up). The reason is by now probably obvious. A state consciousness of Enlightenment is a fully 1st-person experience. It's made of stuff that you are fully aware of in your own immediate experience, and when it does become an actual realization, all of it is fully present in your consciousness and in your experience and in your awareness right now. Nothing is hidden (although you can continue your meditation practice and extend your understanding into more and greater 1st-person experiences).

In this sense, because a human being's immediate experience historically stretches back as far as human beings have had experiences—which is pretty much as long as human beings existed—we can push back cases of Waking Up at least to the shamans' very earliest spiritual experiences (around approximately

30,000–40,000 years ago), which would move the difference in the date of discovery between states and structures from 4,000 years to something more like 40,000 to 50,000 years. This is due to the simple immediate experience, whatever it might be, that is the very nature of 1st-person experience—it is fully and totally present and conscious.

Not so with the complicated, distanced, often 3rd-person nature of structures of consciousness, or the grammar of consciousness, or its syntax. These are all so pre-consciously hidden, with the exception of the very rare ancient rhetoricians, whose full-time job it was to carefully study languages and their grammar and syntax, but none of this was obvious to the typical priest, scientist, doctor, nurse, politician, soldier, or so on—the pattern of basic structures was just not available to most people. In fact, they were not really discovered until around one hundred years ago. A man named James Mark Baldwin noticed that four different knowledge disciplines all underwent evolution or development, and further—and most extraordinarily—they all followed exactly the same stages or levels of development. (He called his universal stages "prelogical," "quasi-logical," "logical," "extra-logical," and "hyper-logical.") Despite the actual names—which focused on "logical" as the center line—Baldwin had two stages prior to logic and two stages after it. But each stage was clearly defined, and what's most important is that with all of the lines that he checked, each of them went through all of those levels in the same order. He checked the Good (or the moral line), the True (or the line of objectively true science), and the Beautiful (the line of aesthetics)—and then added religion, giving four lines in all. But the important point again is that they all developed and evolved through the same basic structures or stages or levels. He mapped this out on a simple graph—with four vertical lines (the four major lines of development) and five horizontal stages or levels (the levels of development)—and thus was born developmental psychology.

Interestingly, while Baldwin was intensely studying *structures*, his good friend William James was very actively studying *states*. He wrote up much of his remarkable research into this realm of Waking Up in the fabulous *The Varieties of Religious Experience*—where religious experiences were all 1st-person totally conscious states. James didn't track their developmental movement very closely; instead, he zeroed in on their goal, and just as importantly, he found that virtually all of the higher forms of mystical religion had essentially the same goal—namely, a direct unity experience of their oneness with God, oneness with the entire universe, oneness with the All. Thus we see profound research into the areas of Growing Up levels (Baldwin) and Waking Up states (James). How fitting they were close friends!

Thus, so far we have *quadrants* (perspectives), *levels* (stages of development), *lines* (various kinds or lines of development moving through the basic structures or levels of development), *states* (different types of Enlightenment or Awakening experiences), and we toss in *types* just to cover the bases (such as the types or lines of development, the types of organic systems found in mammals—digestive, neuronal, circulatory, urinary, sexual, and so on). Thus, there are states, levels, lines, types, and quadrants, falling into the categories of Waking Up (states), Growing Up (levels), Opening Up (to our multiple intelligences or multiple lines of development), Cleaning Up (which we didn't really cover, but it refers to the various forms of psychoanalysis and psychotherapy, all of which aim to re-unite and integrate our split-off and repressed shadow elements with our overall psyche, to produce a whole and healthy psyche or mind), and finally, Showing Up (or fully inhabiting our multiple perspectives—the 4 quadrants). Using all their different epistemologies and ontologies is an act that is guaranteed to give you a very full and very whole integrated view of reality (because you're addressing and including ALL possible views of reality). Using Integral Theory, never again will you get stuck with a partial, limited, fragmented, or broken view of the world. You'll have all of it—the entire universe—at your fingertips, ready to be used in any way that you wish.

As you begin to study this AQAL Framework of complete wholeness—all *perspectives*, all the *levels* or stages of the various structures, the many *lines* of development moving through those stage-levels, altered *states* of consciousness (including Enlightenment and Awakening), and other various *types* of different phenomena—as you study that Integral Framework or become familiar with its various parts, the whole thing will start to rub off on you (and your mind), and you will find that you begin to re-own and reunite and integrate the many psychic elements that you had previously split off and repressed into your mental unconscious. This reunification and integration tends to happen on its own, simply because you are truly thinking holistically, thinking of the world's unified and deeply integrated nature, which you can actually map out on a sheet of paper and thus see it all right before your eyes: oh, there's all the 1st-person stages and lines that I can grow through, and there's the 2nd-person cultural levels and lines. And on the Right-Hand, I can see all the 3rd-person individuals and material things that make up so much of this universe. And look! They all fit neatly together into a UNI-verse, a One Turn Integral Framework. The more that you do that type of integral thinking, the more your own mind begins to take on those characteristics, almost entirely automatically. Of course, you can take up the actual practices of Cleaning Up if you want, and those practices will dramatically accelerate that healing process, since you will be working directly with your shadow material and re-integrating it with the rest of your psyche. This process is highly recommended. But it's all definitely plugging into a UNI-verse, a fully integrated, entire, whole universe.

Well, that's it for a brief overview of the Integral Model and its various elements. I hope this has made sense to you and further demonstrates how to bring politics and polarization into a real

Integral harmony. If you enjoyed this particular application of Integral Theory and want to learn more about using it as a way to navigate these difficult times, then I encourage you to check out my other books.

Thanks a lot, and best wishes to each and every one of you.

Ken Wilber
Denver, CO
November 2023

Selected Books by Ken Wilber

Finding Radical Wholeness: The Integral Path to Unity, Growth, and Delight (2024)

According to Ken Wilber, the perpetual human search for growth and fulfillment is often incomplete. In this book, Wilber integrates the wisdom of spirituality, psychology, shadow work, science, and integral theory to offer us a path to a radical and complete Wholeness of Waking Up, Growing Up, Opening Up, Cleaning Up, and Showing Up. Wilber also includes a discussion of integral sexual tantra. He introduces several practices—on topics such as the witness, one taste, and shadow work—to lead us to direct experiences that we can integrate into our lives. In this way, we truly understand Wholeness and can make room for everything life brings our way.

A Brief History of Everything (2017, 20th Anniversary Edition)

Join Ken Wilber on a breathtaking tour of time and the Kosmos—from the Big Bang right up to the eve of the twenty-first century. This accessible and entertaining summary of Wilber's great ideas has been expanding minds now for two decades, providing a kind of unified field theory of the universe and, along the way, treating a host of issues related to that universe, from gender roles to multiculturalism, environmentalism, the meaning of the Internet, and much more. This special anniversary edition contains, as an afterword, a conversation between the author and award-winning filmmaker Lana Wachowski (*Cloud Atlas*, the *Matrix* trilogy) in which we're offered an intimate glimpse into the evolution of Ken's thinking and where he stands today.

The Religion of Tomorrow: A Vision of the Future of the Great Traditions—More Inclusive, More Comprehensive, More Complete (2017)

A single purpose lies at the heart of all the great religious traditions: awakening to the astonishing reality of the true nature of ourselves and the universe. At the same time, through centuries of cultural accretion and focus on myth and ritual as ends in themselves, this core insight has become obscured. Here Ken Wilber provides a path for reenvisioning a religion of the future that acknowledges the evolution of humanity in every realm while remaining faithful to that original spiritual vision.

Integral Meditation: Mindfulness as a Way to Grow Up, Wake Up, and Show Up in Your Life (2016)

Prepare to encounter your mind in a radically new way as Ken Wilber introduces Integral Mindfulness, a meditative approach based on Integral Theory and Practice. This leading-edge technique combines, for the first time in history, the ancient paths of meditation and mindfulness—or Waking Up—with modern research into psychological development and human evolution—Growing Up—resulting in a complete and powerfully effective method of personal transformation.

The Integral Vision: A Very Short Introduction to the Revolutionary Integral Approach to Life, God, the Universe, and Everything (2007)

An accessible book for anyone who wants an easy introduction to Ken Wilber's thought and its practical applications, both personal and global. The key components of his Integral Approach—a tool for "making sense of everything"—are distilled here into a simple and elegant full-color presentation.

A Theory of Everything: An Integral Vision for Business, Politics, Science, and Spirituality (2000)

A compact summary of the Integral Approach as a genuine "world philosophy," noteworthy because it includes many real-world applications in various fields. A popular choice for introductory reading, it is compact and succinct, with many hands-on examples.

Sex, Ecology, Spirituality: The Spirit of Evolution (1995)

The first volume of the Kosmos Trilogy and the book that introduced the 4-quadrant model. This tour de force of scholarship and vision traces the course of evolution from matter to life to mind (and possible higher future levels), and describes the common patterns that evolution takes in all three domains. Wilber particularly focuses on how modernity and postmodernity relate to gender issues, psychotherapy, ecological concerns, and various liberation movements.

Grace and Grit: Spirituality and Healing in the Life and Death of Treya Killam Wilber (1991)

The moving story of Ken's marriage to Treya and the five-year journey that took them through her illness, treatment, and eventual death from breast cancer. Ken's wide-ranging commentary is combined with excerpts from Treya's personal journals.